Censorship

Censorship

OTHER BOOKS OF RELATED INTEREST

OPPOSING VIEWPOINTS SERIES
Civil Liberties
Education
The Internet
Mass Media
National Security
Pornography
Technology and Society

CURRENT CONTROVERSIES SERIES
Civil Liberties
Computers and Society
Free Speech

AT ISSUE SERIES
Computers and Education
The Future of the Internet
Homeland Security
National Security
Should There Be Limits to Free Speech?

Censorship

Kate Burns, *Book Editor*

Daniel Leone, *President*
Bonnie Szumski, *Publisher*
Scott Barbour, *Managing Editor*
Brenda Stalcup, *Series Editor*

Contemporary Issues
Companion

GREENHAVEN
PRESS®

THOMSON
—————✳—————™
GALE

San Diego • Detroit • New York • San Francisco • Cleveland
New Haven, Conn. • Waterville, Maine • London • Munich

LIBRARY OF CONGRESS CATALOGING-IN-PUBLICATION DATA

Censorship / Kate Burns, book editor.
   p. cm. — (Contemporary issues companion)
Includes bibliographical references and index.
ISBN 0-7377-1580-4 (pbk. : alk. paper) — ISBN 0-7377-1579-0 (lib. : alk. paper)
   1. Censorship—United States—History. 2. Mass media—Censorship—United
States. 3. Internet—Censorship—United States. I. Burns, Kate. II. Series.
Z658.U5C392 2004
363.3'1—dc21
                                                       2003055106

CONTENTS

Chapter 4: Government Censorship

FOREWORD

In the news, on the streets, and in neighborhoods, individuals are confronted with a variety of social problems. Such problems may affect people directly: A young woman may struggle with depression, suspect a friend of having bulimia, or watch a loved one battle cancer. And even the issues that do not directly affect her private life—such as religious cults, domestic violence, or legalized gambling—still impact the larger society in which she lives. Discovering and analyzing the complexities of issues that encompass communal and societal realms as well as the world of personal experience is a valuable educational goal in the modern world.

Effectively addressing social problems requires familiarity with a constantly changing stream of data. Becoming well informed about today's controversies is an intricate process that often involves reading myriad primary and secondary sources, analyzing political debates, weighing various experts' opinions—even listening to firsthand accounts of those directly affected by the issue. For students and general observers, this can be a daunting task because of the sheer volume of information available in books, periodicals, on the evening news, and on the Internet. Researching the consequences of legalized gambling, for example, might entail sifting through congressional testimony on gambling's societal effects, examining private studies on Indian gaming, perusing numerous websites devoted to Internet betting, and reading essays written by lottery winners as well as interviews with recovering compulsive gamblers. Obtaining valuable information can be time-consuming—since it often requires researchers to pore over numerous documents and commentaries before discovering a source relevant to their particular investigation.

Greenhaven's Contemporary Issues Companion series seeks to assist this process of research by providing readers with useful and pertinent information about today's complex issues. Each volume in this anthology series focuses on a topic of current interest, presenting informative and thought-provoking selections written from a wide variety of viewpoints. The readings selected by the editors include such diverse sources as personal accounts and case studies, pertinent factual and statistical articles, and relevant commentaries and overviews. This diversity of sources and views, found in every Contemporary Issues Companion, offers readers a broad perspective in one convenient volume.

In addition, each title in the Contemporary Issues Companion series is designed especially for young adults. The selections included in every volume are chosen for their accessibility and are expertly edited in consideration of both the reading and comprehension levels of the audience. The structure of the anthologies also enhances accessibility. An introductory essay places each issue in context and provides helpful facts such as historical background or current statistics and legislation that pertain to the topic. The chapters that follow organize the material and focus on specific aspects of the book's topic. Every essay is introduced by a brief summary of its main points and biographical information about the author. These summaries aid in comprehension and can also serve to direct readers to material of immediate interest and need. Finally, a comprehensive index allows readers to efficiently scan and locate content.

The Contemporary Issues Companion series is an ideal launching point for research on a particular topic. Each anthology in the series is composed of readings taken from an extensive gamut of resources, including periodicals, newspapers, books, government documents, the publications of private and public organizations, and Internet websites. In these volumes, readers will find factual support suitable for use in reports, debates, speeches, and research papers. The anthologies also facilitate further research, featuring a book and periodical bibliography and a list of organizations to contact for additional information.

A perfect resource for both students and the general reader, Greenhaven's Contemporary Issues Companion series is sure to be a valued source of current, readable information on social problems that interest young adults. It is the editors' hope that readers will find the Contemporary Issues Companion series useful as a starting point to formulate their own opinions about and answers to the complex issues of the present day.

INTRODUCTION

On December 6, 2001, Attorney General John Ashcroft spoke before the U.S. Senate Committee on the Judiciary, relating his personal account of one of the most devastating days in American history:

> On the morning of September 11, as the United States came under attack, I was in an airplane with several members of the Justice Department en route to Milwaukee, in the skies over the Great Lakes. By the time we could return to Washington, thousands of people had been murdered at the World Trade Center. 189 were dead at the Pentagon. Forty-four had crashed to the ground in Pennsylvania. From that moment, at the command of the President of the United States, I began to mobilize the resources of the Department of Justice toward one single, over-arching objective: to save innocent lives from further acts of terrorism.

Ashcroft offered these words to explain and justify new changes in Justice Department policy that were implemented to address concerns about national security following the terrorist attacks of September 11, 2001. Several of the modifications, outlined in the USA PATRIOT Act of 2001, directly affect how the government deals with issues of free speech and censorship.

As the United States entered the war against terrorism under the leadership of President George W. Bush, the American tradition of freedom of expression came under intense scrutiny. This heightened debate over free speech was nothing unusual: A reexamination of First Amendment boundaries has accompanied every war or national crisis in U.S. history. In some respects, the recent reassessment of free speech after September 11 echoes debates from past national emergencies. However, new circumstances and technological advances have added fresh questions that complicate the difficulty of finding a balance between cautious censorship and libertarian free expression.

One of the most controversial provisions of the USA PATRIOT Act is a gag order that prevents the press from reporting on certain FBI surveillance activities, such as monitoring the reading records of public library patrons whom the government deems suspicious. "No person shall disclose to any other person," the law states, "that the Federal Bureau of Investigation has sought or obtained" such records. The U.S. Department of Justice insists that investigative secrecy facilitates timely and successful prevention of terrorist acts. Wartime dangers justify prioritizing safety over freedom, many commentators assert, and therefore law enforcement should be granted increased power to control information. However, organizations such as the American

Booksellers Foundation for Free Expression (ABFFE) and the American Library Association (ALA) maintain that this provision of the PATRIOT Act curtails the public's ability to assess the fairness of FBI investigations that could result in the intimidation or harassment of innocent people. According to these critics, the outcome could be a serious infringement of the right to read books of one's own choosing—a cherished freedom in democratic societies.

This controversy over the USA PATRIOT Act calls to mind previous battles concerning the free flow of information during a national emergency. In the early 1970s, for instance, President Richard Nixon's administration forced injunctions against the *New York Times* and the *Washington Post* to prevent them from publishing what came to be called the "Pentagon Papers," a top-secret report on government deceptions and policies in Southeast Asia that led to the Vietnam War. In the ensuing 1971 Supreme Court case, the Nixon administration defended the censorship in the name of national security during wartime, while the newspapers argued that citizens had a right to know what their government was up to. By a six-to-three vote, the Supreme Court decided against the government injunction because no "clear and present" danger to the nation was apparent. The subsequent publication of the Pentagon Papers helped to fuel growing resistance to U.S. involvement in the Vietnam War.

A marked difference between the 1971 debate over emergency censorship and those that more recently have occurred is the remarkable leap in communication and information technology over the last few decades. While the Pentagon Papers litigation revolved around freedom of information in print, many of the new legal cases involving censorship focus on the dilemma posed by the new world of cyberspace. In the early years of Internet development, it was not even clear whether First Amendment rights extended to electronic communication. Not until organizations such as the Electronic Frontier Foundation (EFF) lobbied to preserve freedom of speech online in the early 1990s did the discussion reach most Internet users.

In terms of enforcing or resisting censorship online during a national emergency, additional questions have to be considered with the old ones. In the first place, the boundaries of the Internet are not equivalent to the boundary lines dividing nations. Which country's notion of appropriate freedom of expression should guide a global technology like the World Wide Web? When users from two—or ten—different countries can meet in an Internet chat room, which nation should have law enforcement jurisdiction? In a forum that makes sharing information so much quicker and easier than before, should special laws apply to disseminating sensitive material electronically? The answers to these questions likely will be deliberated for many years to come.

To complicate issues further, censorship battles during wartime or national crisis have not only occurred in relation to the government, but in the cultural arena as well. A frequently cited example is the blacklisting of artists and entertainers during the Cold War. While Senator Joseph McCarthy and the House Un-American Activities Committee (HUAC) may have led the charge to rid America of Communist sympathizers in the government, it was the Hollywood establishment and other cultural leaders who agreed to enforce the blacklists that put hundreds of actors, writers, and directors out of work because they supposedly held unpopular political opinions. Such extreme measures are often criticized today, yet attempts to censor artists and entertainers still occur in the new millennium. For example, shortly following the September 11 terrorist attacks, Clear Channel, the nation's largest radio station owner, distributed a list of approximately 150 popular songs for disc jockeys to avoid playing on the air. According to Clear Channel, these songs contained lyrics that were too "incendiary, violent, or insensitive" for public consumption. Some applauded the action as an appropriate response to such a large-scale tragedy. Others accused Clear Channel of censoring viewpoints that differed from those of the conservative conglomerate. Arguments over the appropriate boundaries of cultural expression during a national crisis continue to preoccupy Americans as the war against terrorism progresses.

These recurring debates clearly demonstrate that citizens benefit from being well informed about past and present controversies related to censorship. The ability to regulate the dissemination of information is a powerful tool, but it is also a controversial one in a democratic society that professes to be run by and for the people. *Censorship: Contemporary Issues Companion* examines several key censorship issues related to art and entertainment, the media, the Internet, and government regulation. The essays included in this volume illuminate heated struggles over the limits of free expression and the power to censor information. Censorship is a vital issue facing people across the globe today, whether one's country is in the midst of a national emergency, a raging war, or more pleasant and peaceful times.

CHAPTER 1

CENSORSHIP CASE HISTORIES: ART AND ENTERTAINMENT

Contemporary Issues
Companion

A SURVEY OF CULTURAL CENSORSHIP

Herbert N. Foerstel

In the following excerpt from his book *Banned in the U.S.A.: A Reference Guide to Book Censorship in Schools and Public Libraries,* Herbert N. Foerstel outlines major events in the history of censorship from the sixteenth to the twenty-first century. His survey emphasizes contemporary debates over censorship in book publishing, government-funded arts, motion picture production, journalism, education, and the Internet. He concludes that most modern censorship battles are waged over issues of sexuality, profanity, and religion. A noted authority on intellectual freedom, Foerstel currently serves on the board of directors for the National Security Archives in Washington, D.C. His books include *Banned in the Media* and *From Watergate to Monicagate: Ten Controversies in Modern Journalism and Media.*

The issue of banned books has been escalating since Johannes Guttenberg introduced the printing press in 1455. Once speech could be printed, it became a commodity, to be controlled and manipulated on the basis of religion, politics, or profit. After Pope Leo X condemned Martin Luther's *Ninety Five Theses* in 1517, both Catholics and Protestants began censoring materials they found dangerous or subversive. Religious censorship quickly led to political censorship when Luther defied the Pope, bringing an immediate response from Emperor Charles V. On May 26, 1521, the emperor issued the Edict of Worms, containing a "Law of Printing," which prohibited the printing, sale, possession, reading, or copying of Luther's works.

In 1564 the papacy promulgated its *Index librorum prohibitorum* [index of prohibited books], defining those books and authors that Catholics were prohibited from printing or reading. In addition to individual banned titles, the *Index* listed authors whose entire works were prohibited. It also provided guidelines for expurgating books that were generally acceptable and broad rules for the regulation of the book trade. As papal decrees banned new books, the *Index* was revised to keep it up to date.

Protestant censorship followed the same pattern as Catholic cen-

Herbert N. Foerstel, *Banned in the U.S.A.: A Reference Guide to Book Censorship in Schools and Public Libraries*. Wesport, CT: Greenwood Press, 2002. Copyright © 2002 by Herbert N. Foerstel. Reproduced by permission of the publisher.

sorship, with one important exception: Because most Protestant religious leaders accepted substantial state authority over the church, the *state* became the source of most censorship. For example, in England the crown defined heresy, issued censorship regulations, and authorized civil agencies to enforce them. Nonetheless, despite joint efforts of church and state to impose censorship throughout Europe, printed works were surprisingly protected from effective control owing to a clandestine network of distribution. In addition, throughout the sixteenth and seventeenth centuries, Europe's heterogeneity and lack of political cooperation allowed authors to avoid local censorship by having their books printed in other countries.

In the eighteenth century, the breakdown of political power in France made censorship virtually unenforceable. By 1762, when Jean-Jacques Rousseau published the controversial *Émile*, there was a flood of European novels depicting the decadence and debauchery of the aristocracy and monarchy. The police did their best to suppress these books, but without success. In fact, despite the frequent use of police informers to identify the novels and punish their readers, a censored book in Europe was almost always commercially successful.

However, in the United States and England, a social consensus on censorship was emerging that would be far more repressive than overt state or church power. By the 1830s, this new ideology was proclaiming the necessity for propriety, prudence, and sexual restraint. During the remainder of the nineteenth century, private virtue became public virtue, and American and British editors, publishers, writers, and librarians felt obliged to examine every book for crude language or unduly explicit or realistic portrayals of life. In her introduction to the 1984 New York Public Library exhibition on censorship, Ann Ilan Alter said that there may have been more censorship, self-imposed or otherwise, during the nineteenth century in England and the United States than during all the preceding centuries of printed literature. The twentieth century in America has seen the emergence of pressure groups that maintain an uneasy balance in the struggle to interpret our First Amendment rights. The federal government tips that balance in whatever direction the winds blow, and since 1980, those winds have been chilling. Historian Arthur Schlesinger, Jr. notes: "[T]he struggle between expression and authority is unending. The instinct to suppress discomforting ideas is rooted deep in human nature. It is rooted above all in profound human propensities to faith and fear."

The Satanic Verses

Indeed, in the early years of the twenty-first century, faith and fear are still prominent in determining our right to free expression. The most spectacular international act of bookbanning in the twentieth century was surely Iran's death sentence on the British author Salman Rushdie, and America's response to it has not been encouraging. Rushdie went into hiding in 1989 when his novel *The Satanic Verses* offended Iran's Ayatollah Khomeini, who called for his execution and placed a $1 million bounty on his head. The Tehran underground publisher of *The Satanic Verses* had already been killed. "The real book is struggling to get out from under all the rhetoric," says Rushdie. "But I've always said that the best defense of the book is the book itself, when people read it openly and realize that some terrible injustice has been done not only to me, but to the book." Rushdie warns:

> I have tried repeatedly to remind people that what we are witnessing is a war against independence of mind, a war for power. The case of *The Satanic Verses* is, however—and I hope this can be conceded without argument—at present the most public battle in that war. It is a battle that can only be won, because the consequences of losing it are horrendous."

In the spring of 1992, Rushdie made a five-day trip to Washington—his longest time "out of the box," as he put it—to plead for help. The State Department and the White House refused to speak to Rushdie. Margaret Tutwiler, the State Department spokesperson, said there had been no meeting with Rushdie "because at this time we felt that such a thing could and possibly might be misinterpreted." Marlin Fitzwater, speaking for the White House, said: "There's no reason for any special relationship with Rushdie. I mean, he's an author, he's here, he's doing interviews and book tours and things that authors do. But there's no reason for us to have any special interest in him. . . . He doesn't write about government policies."

Political Columnist

Art Buchwald reported a fanciful conversation about the incident with his imaginary White House contact Charlie, who explained the president's snub of Rushdie. "If we let him in to see the President, we risk losing the Hezbollah vote this year. . . . The White House never takes sides between a writer and those who pass a death sentence on him." When Buchwald asked Charlie how we could ignore Rushdie's plight at the hands of the nation that took more American hostages than any other country, he was told:

> That doesn't compare with someone who writes a satire containing blasphemous statements about a religion. The White House disapproves of people being sentenced for what they write. At the same time, you don't rub a book in a nation's face. . . . Americans don't understand other people's cultures. In some countries they kill you for reading a book and in others they kill you for writing one.

In September 1990, the Thomas Jefferson Center for the Protection of Free Expression announced the results of the most comprehensive opinion survey ever conducted on free expression and declared the First Amendment to be "in perilous condition across the nation." The survey revealed that nearly a third of all Americans believe that constitutional protection of free speech does not extend to the media and arts. Robert O'Neil, the center's founding director, cited evidence of an "alarming double standard—a sense that the First Amendment protects what the speaker wants to say, but not equally the expressions of others." Forty-eight percent of those surveyed mentioned some non–national security aspect of the media or the arts in which they felt government should have the power of censorship. Only one quarter of those questioned would support use of their tax dollars to fund art they found offensive. "Obviously," said O'Neil, "Congress is not required to fund any form of art, or to fund art at all. . . . But it is one thing for government simply not to be a patron of the arts; it is quite another for government to say it will support only individual works or artists it does not deem objectionable."

Censorship and Government Funding

The American compulsion to censor government-subsidized expression can be seen in the trials and tribulations of the National Endowment for the Arts (NEA), whose director, John Frohnmayer, was forced to resign in 1992 after he complained of pressure from the Bush administration to function as a "decency czar." Acting chairman Anne-Imelda Radice, appointed by President George H.W. Bush, quickly rejected two grants for exhibits containing sexual themes, overruling the NEA review panels and advisory council that had traditionally judged whether works were appropriate for funding. The next day, Stephen Sondheim, the Tony Award–winning lyricist and composer, turned down the 1992 National Medal of the Arts administered by the NEA. To accept the award, he said, "would be an act of the utmost hypocrisy." He charged that the NEA "is rapidly being transformed into a conduit and a symbol of censorship and repression rather than encouragement and support."

Under overt political pressure from the White House and conservative members of Congress, Radice dutifully testified on Capitol Hill that she would avoid funding sexually explicit or "difficult" work. In an unprecedented protest, the entire NEA peer review panel for visual arts resigned, complaining that the process of peer review had been "severely compromised and placed in great jeopardy." Panel member Susan Krane said, "We have no desire to participate in a puppet process." In another 1992 protest, Artist Trust of Seattle turned down an NEA award, declaring, "Radice's actions are so reprehensible that artists whose work has been approved by the NEA are forfeiting their grants in a show of solidarity for censored artists."

The issue of government funding is increasingly invoked to cloud the First Amendment aspects of censorship. Just as Senator Jesse

Helms can glibly claim that Congress has the right, indeed the obligation, to censor state-funded art in the name of the people, so do various pressure groups insist that the public funding of most schools and libraries makes them subject to "community censorship." This view does not conform to America's cultural or legal history. It may be true that federal and state legislators have the right to arbitrarily withhold funds to the National Endowment for the Arts or to public schools and libraries. But once that money is allocated, whether it be for NEA exhibitions or public library books, we enter First Amendment territory. There is no more constitutional authority to censor public-funded expression than private expression.

At the 1991 annual meeting of the National Society of Newspaper Editors, John Seigentahaler, publisher of the *Nashville Tennessean*, outlined the disturbing results of a national survey on free expression that confirmed the previous year's report by the Jefferson Center. In a 281-page report analyzing the survey, Robert Wyatt, a journalism professor at Tennessee State University, and David Neft, research chief for Gannett, Inc., stated, "After nearly a year of surveying, it is apparent that free expression is in very deep trouble." The report noted that the respondents displayed an inability to distinguish between what the law protects and what they dislike personally. It concluded that Americans display "an alarming willingness to remove legal protection from forms of free expression they disagree with or find offensive. . . . That is, they only believe that they believe in free expression."

Censorship of Educational Material

The 1991–1992 report, *Attacks on the Freedom to Learn*, prepared by People for the American Way (PAW), declared,

> The last several years have witnessed an apparent diminution of Americans' appreciation and willingness to defend freedom of speech and expression. . . . The result has been a series of compromises on freedom of expression, each of which has sent the message to Americans that speech and expression are free, but only within certain parameters. That message, badly at odds with the First Amendment, has fed the wave of curricular attacks in our public schools.

The American public's propensity to suppress expression with which it disagrees is most visible in schools and public libraries, where books are often removed by school and library boards that are vulnerable to local pressure groups. The PAW report revealed that censorship in classrooms and school libraries had increased to the largest single year total in the ten-year history of their report. Some 376 attacks on the freedom to learn, including 348 demands that curricular or library materials be removed, were reported in forty-four states. Nearly one fifth of all challenges to school and library materials came from conservative political groups, some of which have successfully run candidates for school boards.

The count of challenges to materials each year is underestimated, because school systems often seek to avoid controversy by quietly acceding to the censors' demands. PAW notes that, in the past, educators often had to defend their curricular choices against media and lobbying campaigns, including letter-writing drives, petitions, and even paid advertising.

The PAW study found that the three most common reasons for challenging schools' materials in 1991–1992 were:

1. The materials were "anti-Christian," "Satanic," "New Age," or generally contrary to the challengers' religious views. Of the 376 documented censorship attempts in 1991–1992, 140 of them were based on this sectarian point of view. Typical challenges were to books like *Of Mice and Men* and *Catcher in the Rye.*
2. The materials contained profane or otherwise objectionable language. Almost one third of the challenges were on this basis, including books like *The Chocolate War* and *Blubber.*
3. The materials' treatment of sexuality was considered offensive. Over one fifth of the challenges were on this basis, including books like *The Grapes of Wrath* and *Slaughterhouse-Five.*

PAW found that the success rate of the censors in the 1991–1992 school year was disturbingly high, with 41 percent (144 instances) of requests to remove materials succeeding in some measure. During the previous year, only 34 percent of the challenges were successful. "The unfortunate conclusion," states the PAW report, "is that while school systems have grown better equipped to deal with censorship attempts, challengers have more than kept pace in terms of their ability to apply political pressure to achieve their ends."

Government Censorship

The power of pressure groups to suppress whatever they find objectionable is reflected on Capitol Hill where ill-advised legislation imposing censorship on broad categories of expression has dangerous implications for schools and libraries. The badly flawed Child Pornography Act was found unconstitutional in 1989 by a U.S. district court, but a modified version was resurrected during the 1990 Congress. In May 1992, after heavy opposition from the American Library Association (ALA) and the National Association of Artists' Organizations, that bill was also declared unconstitutional by U.S. District Judge Stanley Sporkin for the District of Columbia who said it would chill the exercise of constitutionally protected First Amendment rights to free expression.

Undaunted, Congress introduced an even more disturbing bill, the Pornography Victims Compensation Act (S.1521), which would impose civil liability on commercial producers of "obscene material" if a plaintiff demonstrates that the material "inspired" or "incited" a crime. Thus, a victim of an assault could file suit against a publisher, claiming that expressive material somehow led the criminal to commit the assault. Because of the court's "community standard" definition of obscenity, publishers would have no way to predict what materials a given jurisdiction would consider "obscene" and subject to such a lawsuit. The result would be a kind of prior restraint by uncertainty, with publishers avoiding the possibility of costly litigation by electing not to publish important works.

In a *New York Times* article, Teller (of comic duo Penn and Teller fame) wrote:

> Producers, writers, directors and actors who depict rape are not rapists. They are makers of fiction. To punish them is insane. We might as well punish Agatha Christie for murder and John Le Carre for espionage. . . . It's a death knell for creativity, too. Start punishing make-believe, and those gifted with imagination will stop sharing it. A writer's first thought will be, 'If I write anything original or bold, a reader could get me sued.' We will enter an intellectual era, even more insipid than the one we live in.

The bill did not pass, though it was favorably reported by the Senate Judiciary Committee and actually adopted by the Republican party into its platform. Nonetheless, its sponsors were prescient in anticipating chilling political and legal winds. On May 11, 1995, just a few weeks after a right-wing extremist killed 168 people by blowing up a building complex in Oklahoma City, Oklahoma, a Senate subcommittee held hearings on legislation to criminalize Internet information about bomb-making. Frank Tuerkheimer, a professor at the University of Wisconsin Law School, told the subcommittee that he was able to acquire twelve manuals from the library that contained the same information on bombs that was on the Internet. He noted that the readily available *Blaster's Handbook* tells exactly how to prepare the mixture used in the Oklahoma City bombing.

"I share your concern that there is material on the Internet that I would rather not see," said Tuerkheimer. "[T]here are things in newspapers I would rather not see. There are books I would rather not see printed. However, I believe in a society such as ours, the answer to ideas we don't want to see . . . are ideas that we do want to see."

Senator Dianne Feinstein (D-Calif.) disagreed emotionally with Tuerkheimer. "I have a hard time with people using their First Amendment rights to teach others how to go out and kill and to purvey that all over the world," she declared. Feinstein's sentiment currently pervades the American judiciary, where federal courts, including the U.S. Supreme Court, have recently established the liability of publishers and motion picture producers for the criminal acts of readers and viewers. In *Rice* v. *Paladin Enterprises* (1999), the Court upheld a judgment against the publishers of the book *Hit Man*, after a real-life hit man committed murder following guidelines suggested in the book. In *Byers* v. *Edmondson*, the Louisiana Supreme Court upheld an appeals court decision allowing the family of a clerk shot during a robbery to sue director Oliver Stone and the producers of his film *Natural Born Killers*. The film allegedly "incited" the crime. As the judiciary strikes at the freedom of the publishing industry, Congress has produced a bevy of laws censoring the Internet in ways that may have profound implications for book publishing. In July 1995, the Senate Judiciary Committee convened the first congressional hearing on Internet pornography, at which a number of witnesses urged Congress to take action to control "cyberporn."

Internet Censorship

On February 1, 1996, Congress passed the Communications Decency Act (CDA) and President Bill Clinton promptly signed it into law. The act, which criminalized "indecent" expression on a "telecommunications device" was challenged in court by a coalition that included the American Civil Liberties Union (ACLU), the Electronic Frontier Foundation, and the American Library Association. On June 26, 1997, the Supreme Court struck down the CDA as an abridgement of freedom of speech.

Conservatives in Congress were infuriated by the Court's ruling, and they quickly declared their intention to pass a new, more carefully drawn law. A number of new bills were drafted, but the most popular of these "Sons of CDA" was the Child Online Protection Act (COPA), introduced in April 1998 by Rep. Michael Oxley (R-Ohio).

The COPA retained many of the provisions of CDA, but its sponsors hoped to avoid First Amendment problems by defining the proscribed expression as anything "harmful to minors." The COPA was passed by Congress in September 1998 and signed into law by President Clinton the following month. A coalition of seventeen plaintiffs led by the ACLU immediately challenged the law, and on November 20, U.S. District Judge Lowell Reed granted a temporary restraining order. On February 1, 1999, Judge Reed reaffirmed the restraining order pending a trial on the merits. The Justice Department filed an appeal, leading the COPA down the same path that took the CDA through the federal courts to the U.S. Supreme Court.

A subtle and perhaps more insidious legislative approach to Internet censorship in schools is through the installation of software "filters" on computers that would block student access to inappropriate Internet sites. A flurry of congressional bills were introduced in 1999 and 2000 that would withhold federal funding from schools that did not install filters on their computers. During President George W. Bush's campaign appearances in October 2000, he said he would require libraries to install such filters to prevent children from accessing sexually explicit or violent material. Indeed, a national survey conducted at about the same time revealed that 92 percent of those polled favored filters on school computers to block pornography, and 79 percent said filters should be used to bar hate speech. Behind such support for filters was the more disturbing revelation that 74 percent of those surveyed supported a total government prohibition of online pornography, and 75 percent favored a government ban of online hate speech.

Fighting Censorship

National educational organizations have directed their criticism at federal mandates that would impose filtering on schools, and Internet advocacy groups oppose any form of filtering as an abridgement of First Amendment rights. Marc Rotenberg, executive director of the Electronic Privacy Information Center (EPIC), believes that installing filters on school computers is akin to banning books from a library. "We've described filters simply as censorware," he says. "They can exclude political opinion, medical information and information on sexuality. You essentially rely on someone else's unknown list" to determine what is blocked.

Organizations like the ALA's Office for Intellectual Freedom (OIF) provide an essential public service by documenting censorship incidents around the country and suggesting strategies for dealing with them. Unfortunately, such organizations are finding it difficult to compete with well-financed conservative pressure groups. People for the American Way (PAW) has ceased publishing its highly regarded annual survey of censorship, *Attacks on the Freedom to Learn.* Even the Office for Intellectual Freedom, the nation's best source of news about censorship controversies, announced in its March 2001 newsletter that it could no longer afford the commercial clipping service that provides much of its information. Under the headline "READERS! We Need Your Help!" the newsletter admitted that it would have to place greater emphasis on materials sent in by its readers. It concluded, "Our readers—librarians and free expression advocates nationwide— are now our clipping service."

Despite such budgetary problems, the OIF will continue to document bookbanning and prepare its annual lists of most-banned books. An ironic and unfortunate testimony to the power of banned-book lists was seen during 2000 when a Virginia high school principal ordered teacher Jeff Newton to remove two such lists from his classroom door. Newton had been posting the lists without incident for five years until a parent complained that some of the books on the list had sexual and mature themes. In a letter to Newton, the principal said, "A teacher's door is not . . . a billboard or a vehicle for the promotion of such books." The ACLU intervened, urging the school board to investigate the violation of Newton's First Amendment rights. When the board took no action, the ACLU filed suit on Newton's behalf. In June 2000, Newton resigned under protest after nearly nine years at the school, leading the school board's attorney Douglas Guynn to declare that the case against the school was now "without a vehicle" because Newton was no longer employed there.

Robert O'Neill, director of the Thomas Jefferson Center for the Protection of Free Expression, said, "We felt that constraining a public school teacher's choice of materials, not simply in the classroom, but in this case, materials on the classroom door . . . does in fact abridge a teacher's First Amendment rights." Speaking for the school board, Guynn responded, "He didn't have any First Amendment rights to be violated."

Writers and Censorship

Teachers and librarians are clearly in the line of fire when books are censored, a fact recognized and appreciated by all banned authors. Nonetheless, authors are typically ambivalent about their own role in the principled struggle for freedom of expression.

Kurt Vonnegut, a frequently banned author, says, "I hate it that Americans are taught to fear some books and some ideas as though they were diseases. . . . Well, my books have been thrown out of many libraries. . . . My publisher and I have two agreements on this. One is that we will not seek publicity about the banning of the book. . . . And the other is to see if the individual librarian or teacher is in a jam and whether we can help." Yet Vonnegut admitted that when parents of the "disturbed rich kids" he was teaching in Cape Cod complained of his assignment of *The Catcher in the Rye*, he agreed to change the assignment to *A Tale of Two Cities*. "My job was to teach," he explained, "not to defend the First Amendment." Though most authors may not be so blunt, a surprising number of those I interviewed expressed emotional exhaustion and growing anger at having to divert so much of their time from writing to defending their works, or those of others, against the censors.

In modern society, the censorship of books can be initiated by the federal or state government, by local bureaucrats, or by community pressure. It may occur at any stage of publication, distribution, or institutional control. America's federal government has been inclined to cast its national security veil over massive amounts of scientific, diplomatic, and historical documents, invoking the classification system and export controls to withhold information, the espionage and sedition laws to punish communication, and even prior restraint to prevent publication.

Community Pressure

Today, despite the end of the Cold War, the federal government persists in imposing national security censorship, but the overwhelming majority of bookbanning is local, not federal. Community censorship, particularly in schools and libraries, has targeted books, periodicals, newspapers, films, videos, and even the performance of school plays. This "institutional" censorship prohibits or restricts access to books already published, distributed, and even approved by school or library boards. Such materials may already be on library shelves or part of the teaching curriculum, and the pressure to remove them usually comes from groups outside the institution in question. All too often, the strident demands of a well-organized minority are accomodated by politically sensitive school and library boards or harried teachers. As we have seen, the major grounds for such censorship are sex, profanity, and religion, but they are often intertwined to cover a broad range of "unacceptable" attitudes or ideas.

CENSORSHIP OF NUDITY IN ART, THEATER, AND DANCE

Marjorie Heins

Marjorie Heins presents an overview of the historical censorship of nudity in the visual arts, theater, and dance in the following selection from her book *Sex, Sin, and Blasphemy: A Guide to America's Censorship Wars*. In particular, she compares censorship controversies during the 1960s and 1990s over Broadway musicals such as *Oh! Calcutta!* and *Hair* to examine legal arguments about nudity in art. She traces changing perceptions of artistic nudity during Ancient Greece, the Middle Ages, the Renaissance, and the Victorian era to provide a historical context for contemporary prohibitions of the naked human form. Heins is a lawyer and the director of the Free Expression Policy Project at the National Coalition Against Censorship in New York. She has written several books about censorship, including *Not in Front of the Children: "Indecency," Censorship, and the Innocence of Youth*.

Kenneth Tynan was an iconoclastic British intellectual and theater critic who decided in the mid-sixties that it was about time to upgrade the classic striptease for a more sophisticated audience, and in the process to take a satiric look at the interesting sexual habits of *Homo sapiens*. Tynan asked the American theater director and lyricist Jacques Levy to help him with the idea and put together a high-quality musical revue that would incorporate nudity and test the current limits of sexual freedom in theater art.

In Levy's hands, Tynan's idea began to evolve. Levy recruited an impressive array of international talent to write parts of the script, among them the Irish literary icon Samuel Beckett, the rock 'n' roll poet John Lennon, the satirist and cartoonist Jules Feiffer, and the then up-and-coming playwright Sam Shepard.

Oh! Calcutta!

The finished work was a hybrid, combining dance sequences with skits and jokes satirizing everything from generational differences in sexual frankness to Masters and Johnson–style sex research to differing tastes in pornography. Among the highlights were a coy but restrained opening number that lampooned the traditional prurient striptease, some sophomoric sexual humor, a gorgeous nude *pas de deux* [dance for two] accompanied by a folk music ballad, and other occasional glimpses of well-muscled bare flesh. They called the work *Oh! Calcutta!*—a play on the bawdy French exclamation, *Oh, quel cul tu as!* (Oh, what an ass you have!) With its episodic structure, innovative lighting and design, sequences of nudity, and frankness about sex, the play was a stylistic groundbreaker for American theater.

It opened in New York in 1969, off-Broadway, was a smash success, reopened on Broadway in the mid-seventies and became, for a time, Broadway's longest-running musical. In the late seventies and eighties the show toured nationally and internationally. In the early nineties, it was still touring.

In 1991 the *Oh! Calcutta!* roadshow inquired about booking one of the two municipal theaters in Chattanooga, Tennessee. These are the only two venues in Chattanooga appropriate for staging a big musical. The city said no: *Oh! Calcutta!* could not be staged there. Municipal officials claimed that the show violated city and state "public indecency" laws, and besides, it was legally obscene.

Laws against public nudity or "indecency" are intended to protect citizens from the presumed shock, offense, and embarrassment of being subjected to exhibitionist behavior in parks, subways, or other public places. Chattanooga's idea was to apply these general laws to theater: after all, theaters are open to the public, so it could be argued that the shows performed there take place in "public places." The city thus wanted to use laws intended to protect unwitting individuals from exposure to nudity and apply them to consenting audiences who generally knew what they were getting and didn't mind— indeed, may have come to the show for that very purpose.

Barnes v. *Glen Theatre*

The Chattanooga city fathers took courage in their quest from a recent decision of the U.S. Supreme Court. *Barnes* v. *Glen Theatre*, decided in June 1991, approved the State of Indiana's use of its general law against "public nudity" to ban nude barroom dancing. The *Barnes* decision came as a surprise to the worlds of both art and constitutional law much more because of its reasoning than its result. For in upholding the State of Indiana's requirement that dancers at the city of South Bend's Kitty Kat Lounge wear the minimal coverings of a G-string and pasties, several members of the Supreme Court seemed to use reasoning that could apply equally well to nudity in theater, opera, and ballet.

Chief Justice William Rehnquist wrote an opinion announcing the judgment of the Court in *Barnes*, though only two other justices (Sandra Day O'Connor and Anthony Kennedy) agreed with his reasoning.

Rehnquist started by acknowledging, reluctantly, that nude dancing was a form of artistic expression, whose primary message was "eroticism and sexuality." Nonetheless, he noted, laws against public nudity were part of our history, traceable to "the Bible story of Adam and Eve." The state's minimal requirement of pasties and G-string was justified by its interest in "protecting order and morality," and would "not deprive the dance of whatever erotic message it conveys; it simply makes the message slightly less graphic."

Chief Justice Rehnquist did not explain why he thought this was so. The dancers and their audience certainly might disagree. In fact, artists who use nudity, from barroom dancers to opera directors, probably do so with a specific set of messages in mind. Pasties, G-strings, and the like, may very well interfere.

Oh! Calcutta! provides a good example. As Jacques Levy testified in the Chattanooga case, the idea of *Oh! Calcutta!* was to present human nudity as a symbol of grace, purity, openness, and freedom. Tawdry adornments commonly associated with barroom entertainment are likely to destroy the effect. . . .

Using *Barnes* in Chattanooga

When they denied citizens of Chattanooga the right to see *Oh! Calcutta!* in 1991, the city officials evidently wanted to test the limits of the Supreme Court's ruling in *Barnes*. They also wanted to vindicate their city after its defeat sixteen years before in another Supreme Court case involving nudity. That earlier decision, *Southeastern Promotions v. Conrad*, had concerned the classic 1960s "American tribal love-rock musical," *Hair*. In one brief scene, the cast members of *Hair* strip to their birthday suits in celebration of the Age of Aquarius, but, as critic Lee Mishkin commented in the May 1, 1968, issue of the *Morning Telegraph*, "with all that uproar going on behind, it's probably the unsexiest nude scene ever to have been devised."

Hair encountered censorship problems when it began to tour the country in the early seventies. Sometimes local authorities protested that the show was obscene, sometimes that it violated public nudity laws, sometimes simply that their municipal theater was just like a private one—not open to all comers—and therefore had a right to decide what it wanted to present. In Chattanooga in 1971 as in 1991, the only theaters capable of housing a substantial musical production were municipally owned, and the city simply said no to *Hair*.

Southeastern Promotions, the producer of the show, sued Chattanooga. The company claimed that the municipal theater was like a street or park: owned by the government but open to the public for all manner of free speech doings—a public forum where the government couldn't pick and choose who spoke, sang, acted, or danced there, any more than it could decide which political parties or viewpoints got a permit to hold a rally at the local park.

The Supreme Court agreed. In a major First Amendment decision, the Court ruled that Chattanooga's municipal theaters were public forums, and the city couldn't unilaterally deny access to them. If Chattanooga thought the proposed show unlawful, it had to go to court promptly to get a full, impartial adjudication of the issue.

When Singer Entertainment sought to book *Oh! Calcutta!* in Chattanooga twenty years later, the city sent a delegation up to Nashville, where the show was then on view, to see for themselves. The delegation reported that *Oh! Calcutta!* was really too much for their fellow citizens to handle. Chattanooga's attorneys then followed the procedural requirements laid down in the case involving *Hair* and sued Singer Entertainment. They asked for a court judgment that the show could be banned because it violated both the public nudity and obscenity laws.

The Obscenity Test

Chattanooga's obscenity argument was a bit of a surprise. Under the three-part *Miller* v. *California* obscenity test, a work had to lack serious value, appeal to a prurient—that is, a "shameful or morbid"—interest in sex, and depict sex in a "patently offensive" way before it could be found obscene. Yet it seemed unlikely that *Oh! Calcutta!* could be thought patently offensive by current standards in 1991. It had been a long-running hit on Broadway; it had been presented on tour all over the world and in many American cities; and it was extremely *non-graphic* compared to the books, magazines, videos, R-rated films, and cable TV readily available in most parts of the country, including Chattanooga, in 1991. Its sexual jokes and skits were dated (some were arguably in bad taste), but it could hardly be said that they appealed to a shameful or morbid interest in sex. Finally, *Oh! Calcutta!*'s dance sequences had obvious artistic value. The show had political value in its satires of, for example, Masters and Johnson–type sex research, or married couples trying to revive their failing sex lives. Its scripts had literary value; at least, one might presume this of works by the likes of Samuel Beckett, John Lennon, Sam Shepard, and Jules Feiffer.

But the city argued that times had changed since the unbuttoned sixties. Standards were less liberal now, at least in Chattanooga. At trial, the city's lawyer even argued that *Oh! Calcutta!* promoted sexual promiscuity, which "caused" AIDS; ergo, the show should be banned.

The judge in the case, R. Vann Owens, decided to empanel an "advisory jury." Since this was a civil suit and it sought only a court order, not money damages, no jury was necessary. But the judge evidently wanted to take the community's pulse on the subjective—and touchy—obscenity issue.

Offensive, but Not Obscene

The jurors, after hearing four days of evidence, including testimony by Jacques Levy and other experts, and watching a video of *Oh! Cal-*

cutta!, advised Judge Vann Owens that although they thought the show was patently offensive, they didn't think it was obscene: it had serious value and lacked appeal to prurient interest. The judge reluctantly agreed with their conclusion, but could not resist emphasizing his distaste for the production. "Presumably," he wrote in an opinion shortly after the trial, "the play's overall theme is one of advocating a more casual or relaxed attitude toward sex" (a bit of an oversimplification, but more or less accurate). He went on:

> If the play was intended to advocate freer sex, it was more appropriate in the late 1960s when it was written. The horror of the AIDS epidemic which has resulted from casual sex makes any such advocacy especially untimely today. In any event, however, it is not the popular, intelligent or sensible messages that need the protection of the First Amendment. The guarantee of free speech is *most* important in its role as protector of unpopular and seemingly unworthy messages. Whatever little value the play might have, the First Amendment normally protects against prior restraint where the production is not obscene under the legal test.

To say that Judge Vann Owens missed the point here would be to put it mildly. Sensuality and openness, not promiscuity, is the point of *Oh! Calcutta!* As critic Jack Kroll wrote in *Newsweek* in 1969,

> those who react in anger to the making public of the most intimate of human concerns are missing the point. In a sense all art is about failure and possibility and *Oh! Calcutta!* is evoking the failures and possibilities of our most basic equipment and behavior.

Judge Vann Owens did not ask the jury for advice on *Oh! Calcutta!*'s alleged violation of Tennessee's public nudity law. In his posttrial opinion, the judge avoided this issue by saying that the predicted illegal conduct hadn't yet occurred. There would be time enough to arrest somebody for public nudity if and when it did.

The city never appealed the judge's ruling, so any hopes Chattanooga might have had of retrying the *Hair* case of twenty years before slipped by. *Oh! Calcutta!* played without incident, though with less than a full house, in part because of convoluted ticket sales requirements imposed by the city and strongly encouraged by the judge—to ensure that no minors would get in to the theater. There were no "public nudity" arrests.

An Increasingly Common Trend

Oh! Calcutta! was a stylistic groundbreaker for its use of nudity in serious theater, but Kenneth Tynan and Jacques Levy were hardly alone. By the late sixties and early seventies, nudity had become increasingly common on the European and American stage.

In the Royal Shakespeare Company's 1968 production of Christopher Marlowe's *Dr. Faustus*, for example, the hero's vision of Helen of Troy was embodied in actress Maggie Wright's nude procession, "silent and naked across the stage." Given that Faust's interest in the mythical Helen was sexual, this was "exactly the beautiful vision that Faustus might have had," writes theater historian Gillian Hanson. Similarly, in one staging of Richard Wagner's *Tannhäuser*, the opening scene orgy featured dancers nude except for G-strings, as they simulated a variety of sexual positions; Venus, played by the English soprano Gwyneth Jones, was bare-breasted for most of the show. All this steamy sexuality certainly dramatized the hero's more-than-three-hour struggle to resist the temptations of physical love.

Nudity in Visual Art

If nudity is still a relatively new development in live theater and opera, it's as old as civilization itself in the visual arts. The earliest Greek sculptures, called *kouroi*, were male nudes, and fascination with beautiful, well-proportioned young males persisted through the golden age of ancient Greek culture. Roman artists copied the Greeks, turning out thousands of statues celebrating the beauty, grace, harmony, proportion, and sensuality—but sometimes also the struggle and suffering—that can be expressed by the nude human form.

Christianity changed the nude in visual art and made it an image of shame. Consistent with the Church's view of sexual knowledge as the primal sin, medieval nudes often appeared slouched and guilt-ridden. As scholar Kenneth Clark has written:

> The body inevitably changed its status. It ceased to be the mirror of divine perfection and became an object of humiliation and shame. . . . While the Greek nude began with the heroic body proudly displaying itself in the palaestra [arena], the Christian nude began with the muddled body cowering in consciousness of sin.

The Catholic Church strived mightily to control nudity in both painting and sculpture throughout the Middle Ages and well into the Renaissance. Under Church decrees, nudity was permitted for classical mythological themes but not for religious ones.

Revival in the Renaissance

By the Renaissance, though, Church censorship was becoming a lost cause, as artists began to revive the classical tradition. Michelangelo's *David* is only the most famous of his gorgeous well-muscled male nudes. Donatello's *David* is even more frankly homoerotic in its pose. Caravaggio's males also have a definite come-hither look.

Nor were the glories of the female anatomy ignored. Botticelli's

Birth of Venus is one of the more celebrated examples. Another of the innumerable Renaissance Venuses, by Lorenzo Lotto, has Cupid urinating onto the goddess's naked torso. The notes to this work, which hangs in New York's Metropolitan Museum of Art, explain that it is a marriage painting, and the urine is "an augury of fertility."

The sinewy figures that Michelangelo painted struggling in the throes of *The Last Judgment* on the walls of the Sistine Chapel in Rome were also originally nudes. Pope Paul IV had their private parts painted over with drapery in 1558. Indeed, *The Last Judgment*, despite its brilliance and its religious content, barely survived at all. Another pope seriously considered having the masterpiece destroyed.

Outrage and Prudishness

As the Catholic Church's political hegemony weakened, the naked human form regained its rightful place in Western art, but the ideological struggle continued. From Francisco de Goya's luxuriant *Nude Maja* in 1796 to the palpably sensual women painted by Gustave Courbet, Jean–Auguste Ingres, and others in nineteenth-century France, nudes frequently evoked outraged responses.

The now-common sense of the word "nude" came into use, in fact, as a defense of artists' fascination with the human form against the continuing attacks of church and state. The word was "forced into our vocabulary by critics of the early eighteenth century to persuade the artless islanders that, in countries where painting and sculpture were practiced and valued as they should be, the naked human body was the central subject of art, writes Kenneth Clark."

The semantic distinction, however, didn't always help. In 1769 the Royal Academy of London prohibited any art student under age twenty, unless married, from drawing female nudes from live models. Fifteen years later a nude Venus elicited such outrage in Philadelphia that it was removed from public view. Philadelphia saw some progress in 1806 when the Pennsylvania Academy of Fine Arts presented an exhibit of ancient nude statues and set aside one day for "ladies." Even so, "indecent" statues had to be draped. As Jane Clapp describes in *Art Censorship*, a nude painting displayed in New York in 1815 was denounced as "a deplorable example of European depravity."

Much depended on how a nude was presented. In the nineteenth century, two female nudes by Edouard Manet caused major scandals, not so much because they were unclothed as because of their unashamed, casual, and decidedly contemporary air. *Dejeuner sur l'herbe* shows a naked woman unselfconsciously poised on the grass in a country setting, picnicking with two fully dressed young men. One outraged critic called her "a commonplace woman of the demi-monde, as naked as can be, shamelessly lolling between two dandies." Manet's *Olympia*, obviously a courtesan, evoked a similar reaction.

Fear and loathing of the human nude reached new heights during the Victorian Era in both England and the United States. The new prudery coincided, of course, with enactment of the first obscenity laws in both nations. Under the prevailing obscenity standards, the U.S. government considered any pictorial nudity to violate the law—a view that lasted well into the twentieth century.

Accordingly, in 1933, the U.S. Customs Bureau seized books containing reproductions of Michelangelo's *Last Judgment* fresco in its original nude state. The government notified the art gallery that had ordered the books that it had "detained . . . a package addressed to you containing obscene photo books, 'Ceiling Sistine Chapel,' Filles Michel Angelo, the importation of which is held to be prohibited under the provisions of the Tariff Act." An attorney in the Customs Bureau later ordered that the books be released.

Theatrical Nudity and the Culture War

Nudity cannot be equated with obscenity. It may be brief and fleeting; it may consist only of a baby's buttocks; it may be informational rather than erotic. As British reformer Havelock Ellis noted years ago, it certainly might be presumed that "a young woman of today would possess sufficient anatomical knowledge not to be shocked by the sight of an unclothed fellow creature of her own species."

Yet fear of the unclothed human form remains a mysterious aspect of some societies, including the United States. Today, censorship of theater nudity goes well beyond the occasional fiat by a local government like Chattanooga's. It informs every phase of our culture wars, from government funding decisions to art exhibitions to school curriculums and paintings hanging on classroom walls.

In Charlotte, North Carolina, in 1990, police instructed the Spirit Square Theater that its production of *Frankie and Johnny in the Clair de Lune*, by the American playwright Terrence McNally, could not continue unless a brief glimpse of nudity in the first act was excised. The police said it violated indecent exposure laws. The show's director quickly acquiesced: "Spirit Square is a big organization," he said, "but nobody can afford this kind of legal case."

Frankie and Johnny takes place entirely in Frankie's apartment, where she and Johnny have just made love. The movie version with Michelle Pfeiffer and Al Pacino changed the sets but kept much of the theme—the struggle for romantic commitment in uncertain times. Given that the play is about sexual love, and involves a lot of getting in and out of bed, the brief nudity didn't seem out of order. As the *Charlotte Observer* editorialized, the police mandate was "a flagrant example of using the law to enforce prudish nonsense. . . . Spirit Square is hardly Billy Bob's Beer Joint and Bottomless Emporium, after all, and a law that makes no distinction between the two is a nutty law indeed."

Sometimes, theatrical nudity has been censored without the government's getting involved. Boise, Idaho's Shakespeare Festival in 1991 was to present Frank Wedekind's *Spring Awakening*, a nineteenth-century work about adolescent sexuality and rebellion. When the board of the Boise festival discovered what was afoot, they ordered the director to excise the nudity. He resigned instead. Idahoans never got to see *Spring Awakening*.

Performance artist Karen Finley, who was denied a National Endowment for the Arts (NEA) grant in 1990 because of the controversial nature of her shows, uses nudity for dramatic, rather than pornographic purposes. Finley's nudity as she rages against sexism, homophobia, homelessness, AIDS, and violence against women emphasizes, if anything, the vulnerability, not the allure, of the unclothed female body. But as a result of Finley's radical style, she's widely known simply as the "nude, chocolate-smeared woman."

Resisting Censorship

Not all theaters have caved in to prudery, though. In 1990 the New York City Opera was preparing to present *Moses und Aron*, by the twentieth-century composer Arnold Schoenberg. The opera tells the familiar story of the two biblical characters, the Hebrews' wanderings through the wilderness, and their worship of the Golden Calf. The script at one point calls for "four naked virgins" and a full-scale orgy.

Given then-recent controversies at the NEA, and the New York City Opera's reliance on NEA grants and the private matching funds they are so good at generating, some people began to question whether the virgins in *Moses und Aron* really had to be naked. As critic Peter Goodman reported in the *New York Newsday*, "in the nervousness over offending the religious conservatives who have mounted an attack on the . . . Endowment, City Opera officials worried about the impact of those four virgins." But the result in New York was happier than in Charlotte, North Carolina, or Boise, Idaho: the City Opera overcame its quivers and decided to stick with Schoenberg. Artistic integrity, and nakedness, prevailed.

The same season, the Kennedy Center in Washington, D.C., presented a production of Richard Strauss's opera, *Salome*, also based on a lurid biblical tale. In the story, King Herod is so besotted with Salome's beauty and sensuality that he offers her anything if she will dance for him. It turns out she wants the head of John the Baptist, which, once delivered, she proceeds to kiss and fondle in a manner that would probably meet any censorship board's definition of sexual perversity.

Salome's famous "Dance of the Seven Veils" is often a staging problem for buxom sopranos, but it wasn't for the Washington Opera's star, Maria Ewing. According to published reports, her performance of the famous striptease was utterly persuasive. At the end, critic Octavio Roca wrote, she "stood downstage, naked in bright moonlight, for what seemed a long interrupted climax. It was easy to understand why Herod had promised her anything."

Like the New York City Opera, the Washington Opera wasn't unaware of the risks that a nude Salome created for the company's funding prospects. Ever since 1913, when New York's Metropolitan Opera was pressured into withdrawing a planned production of *Salome*, the work has provoked scandal. Oscar Wilde's play, on which the opera is based, was banned in London when it was first produced. There was considerable speculation in 1990 that, in the words of critic Tim Page, *Salome* "might encounter similar trouble from the Helmsmen"—Senator Jesse Helms—and other "Cultural Commissars."

However, the show went forward without incident—to wild acclaim, in fact. Perhaps Senator Helms and others who had attacked the NEA for funding work no different in spirit but less culturally sacrosanct saw *Salome* as a losing battle.

This did not, however, prevent Helms in 1991 from complaining on the floor of the U.S. Senate about a New York Shakespeare Festival production of *A Midsummer Night's Dream* in which the fairies were all nude or nearly so. Helms failed to note that no federal money had been received for the show. The Shakespeare Festival's longtime director, Joseph Papp, had refused NEA funding after the agency created a requirement in 1989 that recipients would have to sign an oath agreeing not to produce any artwork that might be deemed obscene.

CENSORSHIP IN FILM DURING THE TWENTIETH CENTURY

Matthew Bernstein

A professor of film studies at Emory University in Atlanta, Georgia, Matthew Bernstein has written numerous books and essays about the movie industry. In the following selection, Bernstein traces the history of film regulation from the early government censorship of the 1900s to the "culture wars" of the 1980s and 1990s. He distinguishes between two forms of censorship: official censorship imposed on filmmakers from outside of Hollywood and self-regulation from within the movie industry. Both forms of censorship were often instigated by public protests, Bernstein points out, particularly by pressure groups from religious, ethnic, or other specific communities. Thus, he asserts, the history of film regulation highlights key struggles over cultural values and ideas throughout the history of twentieth-century America.

We currently take for granted the fact that most films made in Hollywood today are created and shown without hindrance. It was not always so. Throughout the history of American movies, there have been countless, often furious struggles to control or influence what could be produced and what could be seen. The cinema has been the most frequent target of the censoring impulse in this century partly because film was the first visual and aural mass entertainment form of the twentieth century, and its power seemed overwhelming. Moreover, film was the most popular mass medium during its first fifty years.

This selection explores some of these many efforts at censorship and self-regulation, in the belief that Americans should neither forget nor dismiss the colorful and varied history of attempts to control the film industry simply because today other media (television, rap music, the internet) occupy what was film's hotly contested position. Movies still generate vigorous controversy from time to time as part of what has come to be called "the culture wars." Moreover, we know a great deal about those historic efforts concerning movies, which have many similarities—and enormous relevance—to current debate about those media. And, of course, we have much more to learn.

Matthew Bernstein, *Controlling Hollywood: Censorship and Regulation in the Studio Era*, edited by Matthew Bernstein. New Brunswick, NJ: Rutgers University Press, 1999. Copyright © 1999 by Rutgers, The State University. Reproduced by permission.

Two Types of Control

Scholars usually distinguish broadly between two kinds of control over movie content. One is external to the film industry. Historically, it took the official form of state and city censors (the film industry called this "local" or "political" censorship), who to some degree reflected a consensus of values and attitudes held by a dominant group in that locale. In cinema's earliest years, official censorship could involve theater licensing. But beginning with Chicago in 1907, it entailed a government body that assessed the moral qualities of particular films—the "prurient" sexuality of Jane Russell's character in *The Outlaw* (1942 and 1946), for example, or the unsettling "social equality among the races" in *Lost Boundaries* (1949).

Often such boards were created in response to public protests against the films, either nationally or locally. Be they women's committees of the teens and 1920s, the Catholic Legion of Decency from the 1930s to the 1960s, or diverse "cultural identity" groups of the 1980s, protest groups could and did bring varying degrees of pressure and persuasion to bear on the movie studios in an attempt to regulate their movie content.

Whatever their provenance, municipal—state or city—civil servants passed judgment on the suitability of movies for audiences. They could excise scenes, shots, or lines of dialogue; or they could ban films outright—such actions are what we typically mean by the term "censorship." The 1915 Supreme Court ruling that movies were not entitled to First Amendment protection provided a legal rationale for imposing prior-restraint on movie exhibition. Films thereby served as an excuse for the public exercise of cultural power, until, with the 1952 *Miracle* decision [which for the first time extended the protection of the First Amendment to movies], the Supreme Court began to undermine the vaguely worded statutes that authorized local censorship. Yet this power was never absolutely secure, nor was it always supported by those it purportedly protected.

A second type of effort at controlling movie content is frequently characterized as "self-regulation." This has taken various forms over the decades. There was the sympathetic advice to filmmakers given—but not enforced—by the National Board of Censorship in the teens. Then there was the more closely observed strictures about representing sex, crime, violence, the professions, and morality generated by Hollywood's trade organization, the Motion Picture Producers and Distributors of America, Inc. (MPPDA) in the 1920s. These guidelines were designed to fend off public criticism of Hollywood. They crystallized into the notorious, though often modified Production Code, drafted by Catholics and revised by Hollywood executives, from 1930 to 1966. Under this latter system, individuals at the MPPDA's Studio Relations Committee (SRC) and Production Code Administration (PCA) intervened in the writing of script drafts and the shooting and editing of finished films from the major Hollywood studios, indicating what might and what would not provoke local censorship against a particular movie and trying to shape films to avoid such consequences.

In fact, this was the primary rationale for Hollywood's self-regulation: the urgent necessity that movies not disturb the political and social status quo in American society or interrupt the flow of box office dollars with controversial material. Even if controversy itself could sell a film successfully in the short run—as with *The Outlaw*, *Blockade* (1938), or foreign films like *The Miracle* (1950)—Hollywood, and the film industry in general, had an enormous stake in maintaining cultural prestige and approval over the long term. And in 1968, as changing values and mores pervaded America, Hollywood's self-regulation became self-classification with the ratings system, developed by the Motion Picture Producers Association (MPAA, successor in 1946 to the MPPDA), which still operates today under the auspices of the major Hollywood producer-distributors.

Society's Reflection in the Movies

What makes the histories of both censorship and self-regulation so fascinating is the various ways in which they expose the fault lines of differing political ideologies, class and religious affiliations, and ethnicities in American culture. Wealthy and influential industrialists objected to Hollywood's portrayal of corrupt coal mining companies (as they did with Warner Bros.' *Black Fury* [1934]); Southern women resented David O. Selznick's insistence on depicting at length what should have been private—Melanie Wilkes's struggle to deliver her child in war-torn Atlanta in *Gone With the Wind* (1939); some African Americans condemned the unconscious racism of Disney's *The Song of the South* (1946), a reenactment of the Uncle Remus Br'er Rabbit stories. Up through the late 1940s, everyone watched the movies faithfully, and many had a great deal to say about what they saw. . . .

Hollywood's desire to stimulate but not to offend audiences and thereby preserve its extensive distribution networks and cash flow can be said to have affected directly what was shown on the screen. This was accomplished through the various negotiations and strategies for representation that arose from industry self-regulation and local censorship. Censorship and self-regulation thus provide the most substantial middle term between various social values and Hollywood film content—and these often unspoken values and ideologies become explicit when controversy erupts over censored and uncensored films.

Hollywood and the Culture Wars

Since the ratings classification era began, filmmakers have enjoyed more freedom than ever before to express controversial ideas or to violate prevailing canons of taste. Yet movie content regulation has continued in new forms. As film critic Charles Lyons has demonstrated, boycotts and protests against movies have continued, particularly in the 1980s culture wars. Feminists, ethnic groups, gay/lesbian rights activists, and Christian fundamentalists all have found particular films of recent vintage offensive (*Dressed to Kill* [1980], *Year of the Dragon* [1985], *Basic Instinct* [1991], and *The Last Temptation of Christ* [1988]); in 1998, Arab Americans protested the depiction of Manhattan terrorists in Edward Zwick's *Siege*. While officially eschewing any program of censorship and claiming only to offer an alternative analysis of the movie in question, the group protests, sometimes at the theater entrance as well as in the media, have often affected a film's box office as well as audience members' interpretation of and reaction to it. It is important to recall as well that since the 1980s, these public criticisms of Hollywood films have occurred while conservative social forces have successfully diminished government support (most notably the National Endowment for the Arts) for the traditional arts.

The 1990s have seen new formations and targets in movie protests. The enormous outpouring of criticism and analysis of Oliver Stone's *JFK* (1991) can be seen as a turf war in which audiences are warned—by journalists, political historians, and various pundits—that filmmakers should not attempt to reenact American history or to dramatize minority interpretations of that history. In this case, the protesting group is not a religious, ethnic, or political association, but a group of related and highly public professions.

Boycotting Businesses

Some protest activists have targeted businesses, not movies, such as the summer 1997 call by the Southern Baptist Convention for a boycott against an entire company, Disney. The SBC was provoked by Disney's tolerant attitude toward gay/lesbian movie and television content (*Priest* [1994], the sitcom *Ellen*) and its employment and theme park policies; the group resented what it called Disney's "Christian-bashing, family-bashing, pro-homosexual agenda." The boycott was to extend to Disney's ABC and ESPN television networks, its theme parks, as well as its films and television shows. While this may account for a chilling atmosphere in Hollywood (evidenced, for example, by the postponed release of Adrian Lyne's 1997 *Lolita*), the SBC boycott has generally been regarded as a failure; a multiform entertainment conglomerate is too diffuse to be vulnerable to the intended effect (members of the SBC might be purchasing Disney products without being aware of it). Yet other constituencies might try refined versions of similar tactics in the future.

Our country's chronic amnesia often prevents us from recalling the past as we confront new problems from technologically based mass media—warning labels on contemporary music, the advent of television ratings, the promise of the television v-chip, and the need for internet regulation most prominent among them. 1998 will be remembered primarily as the year that virtually pornographic accounts of an American president's sexual misadventures were published by mainstream newspapers and became accessible via home computer. While the national and political dimensions of "Monicagate" are unique, this explicitness has provoked considerable dismay and generated many uneasy reflections about what restraints, if any, govern public discourse in contemporary American democracy and regulate the media by which that discourse is conveyed. Such questions revive debates among reformers and protest groups over the movies.

A BRIEF HISTORY OF COMIC BOOK CENSORSHIP

David Jay Gabriel

David Jay Gabriel is the executive director of the New York City Comic Book Museum, which preserves the historical and artistic legacy of comic book culture. In the following essay, Gabriel explains that some of the most fervent censorship battles in the United States have been over comic books. The comics industry enjoyed only a brief period of freedom from censorship from 1934 through the 1940s, Gabriel writes. As comic books became more popular, they increasingly included images of violence and crime, leading many adults to link the reading of comic books with juvenile delinquency. By 1954, threats of government censorship led comic book publishers to establish the Comics Code Authority (CCA) to restrict violence and sexual explicitness. The CCA regulated the industry until the 1970s, when "underground" artists began publishing comics that defied CCA standards. Although the last decades of the twentieth century ushered in the end of official comic book self-censorship, Gabriel notes, at the same time several lawsuits attempted to censor comic books under obscenity charges.

Werewolves, vampires, ghouls, zombies, and cannibals; profanity, obscenity, vulgarity, and nudity; excessive bloodshed, gory or gruesome crimes; depravity, lust, sadism, and masochism, the words CRIME, TERROR, and HORROR; sympathetic criminals, unrealistically drawn females, untrustworthy government officials, humorously portrayed divorces, pleasant criminals, and, above all, evil triumphing over good. In 1955 the comic book industry, fearing government censorship, decided to rid their comics of these—as some claimed—harmful topics, themes, and words. Certainly no violation of any First Amendment rights existed, but the threat to the industry that for years had enjoyed an almost "anything goes" policy dealing with content in their publications, loomed in the foreground during the tumultuous

David Jay Gabriel, "A Brief History of First Amendment Issues in Comic Books," www.nyccomicbookmuseum.org, July 2, 2001. Copyright © 2001 by David Jay Gabriel. Reproduced by permission.

years when senate subcommittees were investigating everything from Lucille Ball to Superman. An industry was forever altered.

The Earliest Comic Books

Famous Funnies was the first comic book sold in the United States in February 1934, and the industry grew from then on. That first book was an anthology of reprinted comics, or funnies, from the daily newspapers. Then in 1935, National Comics published *New Fun Comics No. 1*, an anthology series featuring all new stories. This comic actually ran, in various incarnations, through 1983, when it ceased publication under DC Comics' title *Adventure Comics* (interesting to note that it had reverted by then to a reprint comic). The comics of this early period dealt with just about anything and everything. With limitless imagination, the early comics' pioneers paved the way for future generations of comics aficionados. Stories ranged from westerns, science fiction, mysteries, crime stories, romance, teen stories, funny animals, and eventually—and most lasting—the superhero. As comics matured through the forties, publishers basically relied on "good taste" as their guidelines for what they felt was acceptable to print. This "Golden Age" saw the comic book debuts of such well known characters as Superman, Batman, Captain America, Little Orphan Annie, Dick Tracy, Popeye, Mickey Mouse, Flash Gordon, Terry and the Pirates, the Spirit, the Green Hornet, Archie and his gang, Wonder Woman, and many more characters that would later become firmly entrenched in American popular culture.

World War II brought some important changes to the industry. By the early 1940's, certain comic book titles were selling millions of copies monthly. It was an extremely popular form of entertainment here in the states and with our fighting men overseas. Comic books became increasingly violent to conform to the taste of their audience. And they turned away from the superhero. War, westerns, romance, crime, and horror stories dominated the late 1940's, while parents and educators took notice. Comics were being blamed for robberies, burglaries, murders, suicides, and nearly any other juvenile problem imaginable. Campaigns against comics began to crop up throughout the country, and the Cincinnati Committee of the "Evaluation of Comic Books" reported that "seventy percent of all comic books contained objectionable material, from scenes of sadistic torture to suggestive and salacious actions." A California ordinance even banned the sale of crime comic books to children under eighteen, but a year later was declared unconstitutional. Such bad press led to comics continually being blamed for juvenile delinquency. A band of boy scouts in New Jersey gathered together all the comics they could find and burned them in a bonfire, possibly earning them their eagle badge. Similar events were taking place nationwide, as the country searched for a scapegoat for the problems faced by teens. Some children had comics banned from their homes, sales started to fall for the first time, and a number of states passed legislation prohibiting the sale of comics. As a result of national criticism, publishers, among them Detective Comics (DC), formed an advisory board which included psychiatrists and child welfare experts, the Association of Comics Magazine Publishers. All the while comics became more violent and gory. . . .

The Popularity of Horror and War Comics

Comic books continued to grow in popularity as the 1950's approached. A Columbia serial, *Superman vs. the Atom Man*, helped sales of that book and eventually led to the popular television series, *Superman*, which further boosted the popularity of the comic book. Many new science fiction titles appeared. They included DC Comics' *Strange Tales* and *Mystery in Space*, Marvel Comics' *Strange Tales*, ACG Comics' *Forbidden Worlds*, and EC Comics' (now changed from Educational Comics to Entertaining Comics) *Weird Fantasy* and *Weird Science*. EC's horror comics dominated the scene with *Witches Tales, Chamber of Chills, Vault of Horror, Crypt of Terror*, and *Haunt of Fear*. Even by today's standards these titles are considered gruesome and shocking, with "bloody decapitations, eyes being ripped out, torture, sadism . . . axe murders . . . evil triumphed over good regularly—the kids loved them and the parents and teachers hated them," in the words of Paul Sassienie, author of *The Comic Book*.

There was also a surge in circulation of war titles as America was engaged in the Korean War and many servicemen were still buying comics. Marvel's *Battle* and DC's *Star Spangled War Stories* and *Our Army at War* continued the tradition of the patriotic and often overtly anti-Communist books. *Little Audrey* and *Harvey Comics Hits* featuring Casper the Friendly Ghost and DC's *The Adventures of Dean Martin and Jerry Lewis* dominated the comedy/movie tie-in books. And one of the most significant publications of the decade was EC's humor title, *Tales Calculated to Drive You Mad*, later *Mad*. A few superhero titles remained, but were nearly all overlooked. DC's twelve-year legal battle against Fawcett Comics (DC claimed that Fawcett's Captain Marvel was a copyright infringement of Superman) ended when Fawcett settled out of court. All the while, 3D comics featuring Mighty Mouse, the Three Stooges, and even *I Love Lucy* were huge publishing successes. With horror, war, crime, and other genres of comic books becomingly extremely popular, parents and educators turned a suspicious eye on the medium. The stage was set for one of the most vicious attacks on the comics industry, with either the threat of censorship or the total annihilation of the comic book industry as possible outcomes.

Comic Books as a Threat to Children

The spring of 1954 saw the publication of Dr. Frederic Wertham's book, *The Seduction of the Innocent*, easily the most influential factor in the change in the comics industry. Wertham, a noted psychiatrist and consultant to the Chief Censor of the United States Treasury Department, had an extreme, almost demoniacal hatred for comic books and believed that they were, single-handedly, the cause of juvenile delinquency in the United States. The evil doctor and his devilish tome served to turn society against comic books, and he nearly succeeded in destroying the industry. He wanted comics banned, destroyed, or burned, anything to get them out of the hands of the innocent children who were in all cases (and his findings were known to be half-truths and convenient statistics) addicted to the violence, corruption, and immoral behavior evident in all comics. Wertham believed that children emulated what they saw on the page—suicide by hanging, rape, sexual perversity, murder, flying, shoplifting, and any other odd behavior—and he convinced many people that comic books were the cause. Excerpts from his book reached parents through popular magazines of the time, such as the *Ladies' Home Journal* and the *Reader's Digest*. The country was outraged and concerned as they listened to the "findings" of this determined man. Something had to be done.

In April 1954, the U.S. Senate Subcommittee to Investigate Juvenile Delinquency in the United States held public hearings to investigate the threat comic books had on the youth of America. The hearings were televised and widely reported on in magazines and newspapers. The country was seemingly against comics. Wertham testified, citing numerous examples from *Seduction of the Innocent* which proved conclusively that comic books affected normal children, turning them into criminals, rapists, perverts . . . or worse. He also turned a guilty finger toward the publishers of these offensive books, claiming that they conspired against anyone who threatened them by publicly labeling them communists.

Bill Gaines, EC Comics publisher, and one of the major offenders in Wertham's book, volunteered to testify to help the comics industry. After a series of unfortunate incidents, including his diet medication wearing off leaving him unable to concentrate on the Senate Subcommittee's barrage of questions, Gaines ended up having an opposite effect on the hearings. His answers to certain questions outraged not only members of the subcommittee but also the public. The most memorable was his answer to a question put forth by Senator Kefauver regarding the particularly gory cover to *CRIME SuspenStories #22*, which depicted a woman's severed head being held by a man with a bloody ax. The Senator asked, "Do you think this is in good taste?" Gaines replied, "Yes sir: I do, for the cover of a horror comic. A cover in bad taste, for example, might be defined as holding the head a little higher so that the neck could be seen dripping blood from it and moving the body over a little further so that the neck of the body could be seen to be bloody." Gaines later realized that this might not have been the best answer to this question. It was indeed the final nail in the coffin. The results of the hearings were clear; the Senate's report concluded, "This country cannot afford the calculated risk involved in feeding its children, through comic books, a concentrated diet of crime, horror, and violence." The report made it clear that if publishers wanted to distribute their books on newsstands, then they would have to create a standard, in the form of a code, much like Hollywood had for movies, to keep the harmful or questionable elements out the comics.

The Comics Code Authority

To eliminate any further negative publicity, show their good intentions towards the public and children, and to avoid any repercussions from the Senate, twenty-four of the twenty-seven comic book publishers set up the Comics Magazine Association of America, Inc., on October 26, 1954. The group became known as the Comics Code Authority (CCA). Its purpose was to establish a strict code of ethics, standards, and good taste that all members would abide by. Publishers that adhered to their code would be allowed to print a stamp of approval on the cover of their books, assuring readers, retailers, parents, teachers, and other critics that the material contained inside met the high standards of the Authority and was approved for kids.

Wertham denounced this self-regulatory response, and fans claimed it brought the death of their beloved comic books. Many believed that censorship was censorship no matter what form, and in the end it would be the art that would suffer. In order to ensure distribution to newsstands, at that time the only method they were sold, comic books needed that stamp of approval. Most publishers complied and produced "post-code" comics that were bland and infantile. Dell Comics used their own code with some small success. EC Comics soon after replaced all of their offensive, highly popular books with less than popular comics, with stories of pirates, science, and medical stories. However, an argument soon erupted between Gaines and officials of the CCA over whether a black character in an issue of *Incredible Science Fiction* could be drawn as having beads of sweat appear on his brow. The CCA claimed this was a racist depiction and wanted the sweat removed. Furious, Gaines refused and decided that was the end of the code for him and his books. Gaines eventually left the group that he was instrumental in forming. Within a year, the only remaining EC title was the groundbreaking *MAD*, which started printing in black and white magazine format and became the biggest selling humor magazine of all time.

Despite the regulations of the code, two states adopted laws to regulate comic books. The Comic Book Act was passed in Washington State in 1955. This act made it illegal to sell, or possess with the intention to sell, comic books without a license and required dealers to send to the Division of Children and Youth Service of the state three copies of each comic book they planned to sell. The second ordinance was adopted by Los Angeles county and prohibited the sale or circulation of crime comic books to minors under eighteen. This ordinance also defined a comic book as a series of five sequential drawings with narration. Both laws were soon after declared unconstitutional. . . .

The late fifties brought many changes to the face of the comic book industry. Many publishing companies went out of business. Atlas, Ace, Superior, Quality, and some others sold off characters to other companies, all a result of the infamous code. Marvel cancelled over fifty titles and faced increasing financial hardships. Yet, the aftermath of the code and the end of the fifties brought some familiar characters into the comic book universe. Characters like Little Lotta, Little Dot, Richie Rich, Baby Huey, Jackie Gleason, Sergeant Bilko, Lois Lane, Superboy, a new Flash and Green Lantern, and ultimately the Justice League of America—a reworking of the first and greatest superhero team of comics' Golden Age, the Justice Society of America—emerged from this stagnant period. These characters ushered in comics' Silver Age. The sixties would prove to be full of their own First Amendment issues.

The Silver Age

In the early sixties, comic book companies surged ahead, overcame their limitations as created by this self-censorship, and moved ahead to new heights of glory, especially Marvel Comics, the company credited with reinventing the comic book superhero and super-team with the *Fantastic Four*, the *Amazing Spider-Man*, the *X-Men*, and many other titles and characters. Inspired by the comics, popular TV shows *Batman* and *The Green Hornet* renewed fan interest and brought a new generation of readers. Not only did the major companies thrive, but also a strong "underground comix movement" had formed, led by cartoonists like Robert Crumb, Gilbert Shelton, and Robert Williams. These artists produced an acclaimed body of adult-themed comics that dealt with taboo subjects of interest to their counterculture, specifically sex and drugs. While no real threat to the commercial comic book industry, these underground artists were able to escape the constraints of the Comics Code as their works were distributed through mail order, alternative record stores, head shops, and directly from the artists. Although the creative freedoms may have been envied, the eventual decrease in the popularity of the counterculture, rising production costs, a wave of obscenity prosecutions, and the closing of head shops as a result of anti-drug laws across the country, led to a marked decline of the underground comics. . . .

Breaking the Code

By 1970, the highest selling comic book in the country was *Archie*, selling nearly 500,000 copies a month. Sales were declining for most publishers as readers once again lost interest in superheroes. The talented team of Denny O'Neil and Neal Adams, instrumental in decamping Batman after his trivialization on television, turned to the characters of Green Lantern and Green Arrow, DC mainstays throughout the Silver Age. O'Neil attempted to infuse stories with his own commentary on the problems of the 70's, including ecology, overpopulation, racism, sexism, and due process of the law. They examined all these outdated issues of the code except drug abuse. The code still forbade the depiction of drugs in comics. The stories were hard hitting and highly acclaimed, but did little to boost sales; although today these are some of the most valuable and sought after books of the period. However, it was Marvel Comics and its youthful hero Spider-man who finally broke the code. In 1971 Stan Lee, head of Marvel, received a letter from the Department of Health, Education and Welfare asking for a Spider-man story portraying the evils of drugs. Lee agreed that it was an important issue for his character to combat, and *The Amazing Spider-man #96–98* dealt with a character overdosing on drugs. The books were distributed even though they did not receive the Comics Code Seal of Approval, and yet fan and public reaction was extremely positive. Said Lee, "everybody loved what we did. And because of that, the code was changed." Incidentally, DC eagerly followed suit with *Green Lantern/Green Arrow* drug issues.

The code was revisited after 17 years in late 1971, and its policies and standards were altered to allow more lenient story approval in the future. This heralded the return of vampires, werewolves, and zombies to the comic book page. Publishers were quick to try to recapture the days of the horror comic and almost overnight ushered in titles like *Werewolf by Night, Tomb of Dracula, The Demon, Swamp Thing, The Monster of Frankenstein, Tales of the Zombie, Vault of Evil,* and *Forbidden Tales of Dark Mansion.* Marvel even was able to introduce the first black superhero comic, *Hero for Hire, Luke Cage,* without fear of racist outcries. An era of renewed creative freedom existed throughout the comic book industry, and all was better in the comic book world. . . .

The Maturation of Comics as an Art Form

The 1980's saw many new developments in the comic book market. DC and Marvel capitalized on the popularity of many of their characters through mini and maxi series; and toy tie-ins like *G.I. Joe, He-Man and the Masters of the Universe, Rom,* and the *Micronauts* were also successful. One of the biggest merchandising phenomena was Mirage Studio's *Teenage Mutant Ninja Turtles,* with everything from clothing, toys, films, and even an animated television series. Marvel once again revolutionized the industry with their adult line, Epic Comics (which brought the highly successful Japanese manga title, *Akira,* to American audiences), a hugely successful graphic novel in 1982, *The Death of Captain Marvel,* and the rise of the X-Men with spin-offs, new series, miniseries, and graphic novels for their much loved Mutants. Comics continued to push their own boundaries while developing into a more mature, highly profitable, art form. However, not everyone appreciated this new sophistication as certain religious and conservative leaders decried these developments, claiming that "comics are for kids."

While mainstream comics were enjoying their success, a new group of "alternative" comics arose. By 1983 there were more publishers than there had been in nearly forty years. These publishers relied on the direct sales market to sell their product to the public, an idea inspired by the underground artists. The success of ambitious publications such as *RAW, Love and Rockets, American Splendor,* and *Elfquest* created by such talented individuals as Art Spiegelman, Dave Sim, Will Eisner, and Wendy and Richard Pini were a result of the talent and dedication of their creators. Eclipse Comics followed up their successful graphic novel of the late seventies, *Sabre* (reportedly the first graphic novel ever to be sold on the direct market), by giving the character his own series. First Publishing obtained the rights to publish the internationally acclaimed Japanese comic, *Lone Wolf and Cub,* while more translated versions of *manga* comics began to appear on the American comic market. The industry was booming, but not devoid of problems.

In 1986, Friendly Frank's, a Lansing, Illinois, comic shop was charged with selling "obscene" comics. A minister had entered the store after seeing a life size stand-up display of Wonder Woman; he claimed it looked satanic. He soon discovered the adult section, with titles such as *Omaha the Cat Dancer,* the *Bodyssey, Weirdo,* and *Bizarre Sex.* The store manager was arrested, not for selling obscene material, but merely for making it available in his store. Friendly Frank himself, the owner of the store, contacted his friend Denis Kitchen, the publisher of several of the questionable titles. Denis contacted friends of his, and together they put together a portfolio to fund the defense of the store manager. With the aid of this "legal defense fund," the case moved to the Appellate Court, and the manager was acquitted of all charges. Realizing the value of this venture, the Comic Book Legal Defense Fund (CBLDF) incorporated to support the defense of First Amendment rights of comic book creators and retailers. Their work continues.

Then, in 1989, the Comics Code had yet another revision. The measure was undertaken to give the code a more "contemporary wording and interpretation," according to Amy Kiste Nyberg, author of *Seal of Approach: The History of the Comics Code.* Basically, the code still existed for books that appealed to a mass audience and continued to assure parents that they were suitable for children. Comics targeted for adults would not carry the code on their cover. This revised code replaced the older version's more specific rules and standards with general guidelines on language, violence, characterizations, substance abuse, crime, attire, and sexuality. These were outlined for use by publishers, editors, and artists and were "forbidden to be distributed to members of the press or general public," Seal writes. This was pretty much the end of the Code as a symbol of any outside authority and a marked decline of the repression of censorship. The Code remained on many comics, despite the fact that most readers, and some industry professionals, did not even know what it was for. More and more companies would emerge utilizing the direct market only. Without the need for newsstand distribution, there was no need for a Code. . . .

Recent Developments

The 1990's saw interesting developments in the comics industry. These were the years of the "gimmicks" comics: hologram, multiple, die-cut, foil-embossed, and glow-in-the-dark covers, trading cards giveaways with purchase, Deaths, Returns, new universes, TV (live action and cartoon) tie-ins, creator-owned comics, clones, multiple X-titles, and on and on, the concentration seemingly being on dollars and not content. Movies based on comics brought huge interest in comic-related merchandise, translating into dollars for publishers. Movies like *The Teenage Mutant Ninja Turtles, Batman* (the most publicized film of 1989 had a slew of sequels), and a comic from the thirties was once again on the silver screen when the much-anticipated *Dick Tracy* opened in 1990. Mickey Mouse comics were the first to appear in Russia in 1991. Jeff Smith's *Bone*, a character reminiscent of Wait Kelly's *Pogo*, was a refreshing addition to the industry.

DC, Marvel and Archie Comics were the only companies still publishing comics under the self-censoring code, a vestige of the fifties that continued to hang on. Image Comics, a completely creator-owned company whose creation was the biggest news of the decade, remained free of the Comics Code stamp of approval, as did many other independent companies. In 1993 DC started its "mature" line of comics, the Vertigo imprint, producing horror, mystery, fantasy, and some superhero titles. Vertigo books were also liberated from the code's restraints with an "intended for mature audiences" tag on their covers.

Into the Twenty-First Century

But even as the comic book industry progressed toward the Millennium, obscenity cases continued to crop up around the country. Two typical cases revolved around Florida comic shops, one selling the adult collection, *Cherry Anthology #1*, to an undercover police officer, and the other for selling a "mature" book, *The Score*, to an underage boy accompanied by his mother. Both stores, assisted by the Comic Book Legal Defense Fund, were acquitted of all charges. . . .

In 2001, Marvel Comics decided to take a bold new step in their publishing decisions and announced that they dropped the code altogether. Instead of the antiquated standards and regulations, they have their own rating system, just like movies and television. Without the fear of Senate censorship, book burnings, hearings, bans, trials, sub-committees, or seducing any innocents, Marvel has concluded that the standards of the 50-year-old Comics Code "are just inappropriate for our consumers and our retailers and our business in the 21st century." Said comic book artist Frank Miller, a strong supporter of First Amendment rights "Losing the code? That can only be a good thing. I'd rather they just kill it and didn't replace it with anything. Who needs this nonsense—or these leg irons?"

The history of comics is fraught with scares, threats, and even denials of First Amendment rights. Obscenity cases crop up by the dozens for the CBLDF to fight, and many involve the First Amendment rights of comic book creators. Attempts have been made to pass laws regulating, banning, or censoring comics, and they have all been found unconstitutional. Institutions all across the country continue to deny retailers and readers the right to read, purchase, or sell any book that they might find obscene or offensive. A denial of First Amendment rights still exists loosely in the form of the Comics Code. But that is rapidly changing as the last vestiges of the Code's artistic restrictions are almost all nearly gone or forgotten. Marvel Comics is taking the lead against the Code by removing it from their books and returning to creators their absent artistic freedom. While Wertham's influences may nearly all be gone, the comic book industry should remember the precious gift that has been retrieved: the gift of the freedom of speech, unhampered by the public, unchanged by their peers, and unregulated by the government.

CHAPTER 2

CENSORSHIP IN THE MEDIA

SELF-CENSORSHIP IN BROADCAST TELEVISION: AN OVERVIEW

Alfred R. Schneider, with Kaye Pullen

Alfred R. Schneider is an attorney and a consultant in the communications industry with many years of experience in the broadcasting business. Formerly the vice president in charge of administration for the ABC television network, Schneider served on the National Association of Broadcasters' Code Review Board for twenty years. In the following selection from his book *The Gatekeeper: My Thirty Years as a TV Censor*, Schneider chronicles the controversies related to television content and freedom of expression that spanned his career. He notes that standards concerning appropriate depictions of violence and sexuality for both adult and children viewers changed immensely from 1960 to 1990. Television censors have the difficult task of balancing the needs and concerns of viewers seeking entertainment and education, public and private groups advocating quality programming, and broadcasting companies hoping to make a profit, Schneider concludes.

During thirty years of tumultuous social and political change, I was chief censor of entertainment programming for the American Broadcasting Company. From 1960 to 1990, as one of three independent, competitive gatekeepers, my decisions shaped the texture and taste of television programs that eventually reached 90 million homes. In this retrospective of the battles, occasionally waged frame by frame, over program content, I trace the evolving, sometimes accelerating changes in our national life as reflected on the television screen.

What was once sexually daring is now prosaic, and yesterday's blood and gore is now tame, but even in today's freewheeling media environment, familiar issues, with which I once grappled, remain in play: Does violence on the screen, large or small, breed real-life violence? Should children be protected from the influence of the media? And if so, how? Which demands from special-interests groups are valid? What is the role of the censor in a free society?

In the invisible but unique role I played behind the stage in television, I answered such questions in different ways at different times. This is the inside story of my experiences as censor in what often seemed a quixotic quest to maintain an appropriate equilibrium for television entertainment programming as new social and political issues, such as civil rights, feminism, homosexuality, euthanasia, and sexual abuse, emerged. The pace of social and political change was also matched by changes in the media marketplace as the dominant three networks faded into the multi-channel media universe.

The tensions in this ongoing drama were not only between the producers of programming and the networks with all the attendant economic pressures, but were also from the forces brought to bear by government, industry watchdogs, the public, and a chorus of special-interest groups. Unlike insider stories of other corporations, this one deals with the images, ideas, and fantasies that dominated the public airwaves: a diary of our lives.

Early Television Scandals

It begins in the late 1950s when scandals erupted over quiz shows and payola. When the public learned that those sweating contestants on such television game shows as *Twenty-One* and *The $64,000 Challenge* had received the answers in advance, an uproar ensued. The other deception primarily involved disc jockeys who accepted payment to play records instead of selections based on sales records or merit.

When the government and public attention came to bear on network executives, they reshaped the industry in ways that directly affected my future. In January 1960, after a brief stint at CBS, I returned to ABC Television Network as vice president of administration. One of my first mandates from an unhappy Leonard Goldenson, president of ABC, was to see that he never again suffer the embarrassment of having to defend himself before a congressional investigating committee.

Goldenson had been called to testify about ABC's relationship with Dick Clark and Clark's receiving money from an airline in exchange for an on-air mention. At the time, there was no legal requirement for such disclosure, but in the climate of scandal it came to be looked upon as another form of deceiving the public.

In the unhappy glare of public and government criticism, each of the networks, ABC, CBS, and NBC, took direct control over entertainment programming and expanded their departments of broadcast standards and practices (BS&P). From that point on, every script, every program, live, film, or tape, was to be scrutinized by an editor for taste, accuracy, violent portrayals, and sexual overtones. This far-reaching review did not apply to news, documentaries, or sports, where the traditional rules of journalism governed. Eventually, that strange mixture of fact and fiction, the docudrama, would create a new programming category, which required the adoption of some of the news department's practices and guidelines.

Television in the 1960s

The network's censorship of entertainment programming began in one of the most tumultuous decades of social change in American history. Political debates took to the streets, and the pattern of family life began to shift in ways that continue to reverberate. Innovation, experimentation, and exploration were the buzzwords in television programming as the adolescent medium grew up along with the nation. Television itself became the lightning rod for many controversies about what was happening in society.

Was television a "vast wasteland" corrupting the values of the young? How did television affect children's behavior, their attitudes, their reading scores, their perception of the world around them? The underlying question—what was the medium doing to us?—is asked about any medium, but with television and its intimate reach into the home, it took on a new urgency.

In the 1960s, Congress began to hold hearings on the effects of television violence and a substantial part of my thirty years at ABC was spent worrying about how to treat violence. To me, it's ironic that while opinion leaders, members of Congress, educators, sociologists, and children's advocates intensely debated and tried to determine cause and effects of depictions of violence, the viewing public largely remained untroubled. Regional differences did appear on violence as well as other issues, but the gap between what the viewers watched and the opinion leaders debated created a territory where producers gained important leverage.

The public might have been blasé, but government officials in a continuing series of hearings and other pressure-making initiatives shaped the public debate and the headlines, and raised concerns within the industry. . . .

The late Sen. John O. Pastore asked, "Even if only one child is affected by watching violence on television, don't you think you have a responsibility to do something?"

Negotiating TV Violence

The government, broadcasting's landlord, so to speak, raised issues in the public forum, and, inside the house, the battles began with the producers. Programs such as *The Untouchables, Combat*, and *Mod Squad* all required tough negotiations to retain the action format but decrease the body count.

To give a flavor of this sustained, unremitting debate over appropriate violence, I recall two hours in a room with producer David Wolper and Brandon Stoddard, program executive in charge of ABC miniseries, counting the number of lashes in the whipping of Kunta Kinte in *Roots* and raising questions about how many scenes in an hour could contain violence in *The Mod Squad* or *The Rookies*, and if humor mitigated the impact of violence. How should slow motion be used? Would slow motion footage make *The Six Million Dollar Man* acceptable for 8 P.M. on Sunday?

ABC, CBS, and NBC each set up social research departments and conducted independent research on the effects of television violence on the child viewer. We were called to testify almost every year from 1962 to 1972. The battle to entertain, to capture an audience, to portray conflict, and to eliminate gratuitous and excessive violence was joined. It culminated in the ill-fated Family Viewing Hour.

Sex on Television

The noisy debate over violence often was drowned out by equally vociferous complaints about the portrayal of sexuality. Congress and other public voices blamed television for sexual promiscuity, the breakdown of the family, premarital sex, and adultery.

While the 1960s roared on with increasing sexual permissiveness, our BS&P editors had to contend with the strange American dichotomy between what's acceptable in private behavior but not to be acknowledged or depicted on the television screen. The sexual times indeed were changing, but how much of that was "appropriate" in entertainment programming? Many a call by editors could be designated arbitrary and capricious, and many once "controversial" topics are today's routine programming fare. In the late 1960s and early 1970s, television began to treat such topics as adultery, premarital sex, pregnancy (at first without use of the word), and abortion, but not without sometimes protracted negotiations about the actual presentation.

Year by year, program by program, in comedy and drama, television programming ventured into more and more controversial and sensitive subjects in the arena of sex. Often, a theatrical movie or a made-for-television movie would push the limits of acceptable content or language. Series programming would follow and similarly push the envelope. At other times, a drama such as *Something About Amelia*, with its theme of father/daughter incest, was developed especially for television. For that 1983 broadcast, ABC provided a caller "help" line.

The Role of the TV Censor

Besides having nitty-gritty battles with producers, I was asked to explain or defend my decisions as the censor to the network's affiliates or before industry panels. An important part of my role was to listen and learn from public and industry debates to frame a flexible standards and practices policy, but my bottom line was: the realities of commercial broadcasting. Working in a highly competitive industry, my objective was to keep entertainment programming responsive to change without forcing unwanted change on the viewers. The attainment of the objective was often subject to circumstance, the times, and several conflicting factors. Was I to be a conduit of viewer reaction or of advertiser desire or of special-interest advocacy, or was I to be the opinion maker? Could I free myself from the will of commercial and governmental interests and truly be the conscience of the corporation? How does one reach reasonable and valid decisions for a new medium where few knew what would succeed, let alone determine what would be acceptable program fare reaching into the private living rooms of America? "Censor" was a dirty word to those First Amendment devotees, but it was a mandatory function for those who saw evil in the forces of the controllers of content in this new medium. My role as censor developed and changed along with the substance and style of entertainment programming during thirty years.

Perhaps "gatekeeper" better describes the function of the television censor. When new doors are opened, and taboos broken, the censor holds the key to standards of entry or passage. There are no better illustrations of the dynamics of change than the confrontation we had with Woody Allen when ABC purchased his motion picture *Annie Hall*, or the caustic sessions with the late Richard Brooks over edits in his *Looking for Mr. Goodbar*, which occasioned a change in a long-standing policy of requiring the Motion Picture Association of America (MPAA) to review our edits and rerate R pictures.

After editing *The Last Picture Show*, in the fall of 1974 on a Moviola on a back lot in Los Angeles, with Peter Bogdanovich on one side and Andre de Szekely, our creative editor, on the other, I vowed I would never again subject myself to such tension and stress. Bogdanovich resisted our editors' cuts, and the only solution was to sit and negotiate frame by frame our cuts and his reluctance. Editing theatrical movies for television was a chore that cable never faced and today's broadcaster finds less of a burden.

Broadcasting Controversial Social Issues

Is it strange or hypocritical to mention freedom of expression in the same breath with censorship? Maybe, but censorship in television sometimes creates strange alliances. Often, our role was to try to see how to help get the program on the air rather than just say no.

Probably a turning point in both television acceptability of program content and the audiences awakening to a hidden problem in our society was a movie of the week, *Something About Amelia*, the story of father/daughter incest. Producer Leonard Goldberg convinced Brandon Stoddard in ABC Programming that he could deliver a movie within acceptable boundaries. Goldberg and I found the way. Movies of the week, MOWs, were introduced by Barry Diller early in his career in the programming department.

Motion pictures originally produced for theatrical presentation were becoming more expensive, as each network bid higher license fees for top product. Barry created the ninety-minute movie as an economic and entertaining substitute, and promoted it as he would a motion picture bought for television viewing. He sought provocative and controversial subjects that broke down barriers to topics and treatment.

For example, *That Certain Summer* was the first full-length television drama about homosexuality. The movie won critical acclaim and distinguished the movie of the week as a hit weekly series.

Children's Television

High on the BS&P agenda were programs designed for children. One of the motivators and leaders in the battle for programs designed for children was Peggy Charren. The founder of Action for Children's Television (ACT), she focused her attention, and ours, on when was television going to give children the healthy, educational, "pro-social," entertaining programs its public-interest responsibility dictated.

Saturday morning, weekday, and programming designed primarily for children and teenagers became the target. In the mid 1970s, the term "pro-social" set a standard for program content in these categories.

Academic researchers, the PTA, and the baby boomers of the 1950s who were beginning to raise their own families took interest. The responsibility of the media, they said, was not only to ensure that children were not harmed, but also to help children develop skills and values conducive to positive mental growth. Children's programs should deal with sex roles, role modeling, ethnicity, and stereotyping.

All this "goodness" and conscience, however, had to be placed within the framework of a commercial broadcasting system governed by the economics of free enterprise. We could not just educate. We had to educate, entertain, and sell.

Of prime concern, then as now, was the effect of Saturday morning cartoons. Not until the late 1960s were animated cartoons created primarily for television. Earlier cartoons were made for theatrical distribution and catered to both an adult and child audience. Filled with violent action, stereotypes, white- and male-oriented, they became the subjects of critical disdain, and various writings espoused their behavioral harm on young minds. A controversy emerged between those who argued violence is violence in whatever form and those who excepted comedic violence from the potentially harmful category.

Michael Eisner, now chairman of Walt Disney, then head of Saturday morning children's programs at ABC, came to the office to seek acceptance of the new *Superfriends*, a version of Superman and Batman in action-adventure cartoons. Was *Superfriends* an opportunity to affect a child's perception of sex roles and role modeling? You bet it was! *Superfriends* would introduce the first woman superhero, Wonder Woman, along with black, Asian, and Indian superheroes as role models.

In 1972, ABC began an afternoon series of one-hour specials that reached deeply into the quality of life for young teenagers. All the programs in *The ABC Afterschool Specials* had one goal: to respect the needs, intelligence, and sensitivity of children.

Throughout these several decades, there were conscious efforts to meet the intelligent and valid criticism of programs for children. It was an enlightened era in which we sought to brighten the horizon of young people.

Blaming Television

To participate in change, as I often witnessed, requires courage and stamina. Frequently, television was the scapegoat and was sometimes simply caught in the cross fire of cultural wars. The public, elected officials, individual station operators and management, and the advertising community all looked to the networks to meet and answer the frustrations of the time.

Stop destroying the moral fiber of the nation, some cried. Set standards to hold back the tide of change, others insisted. At the same time, the networks had to respond to the voracious appetite of viewers for new and diverse programs; most of these viewers seemed ready for changes in programming content. One facet of the censor's job became to serve as a gatekeeper of values and morals, as arbiter of good taste, as judge of fairness. The censor was to listen to the pleas of the conservative, religious, and cultural elite interests. On the other hand, he was not to turn away from the liberals, civil libertarians, feminists, and ethnic and social constituencies seeking similar opportunity to influence the viewer.

I had many experiences with the numerous special-interest advocates who wanted their voices heard on television or their point of view presented in programming. Returning from a short lunch one afternoon in the middle 1960s, I learned a homosexual activist group had taken over Leonard Goldenson's office to protest an episode of *Marcus Welby, M.D.* This was the first of many clashes with the homosexual community. While most confrontations with special-interest advocates were not as dramatic, the necessity to listen and respond to divergent interests occupied much of my time and energy.

Television matured and so did viewers, who became more sophisticated not only in their viewing, but also in their tactics to get a response from the industry. Morality in Media held hearings about family values; the Reverend Donald Wildmon formed fund-raising groups to sustain attempted boycotts on advertisers who sponsored programs that they felt should not be telecast. This is also part of the story.

Besides my role at ABC, I served along with several station representatives, some affiliated with networks, others from independent stations, on the National Association of Broadcasters Television Code Review Board. Its function was to serve as the legislative and judicial body governing industry compliance with a code of principles and guidelines. The code was in addition to rules of permissible entertainment programming under which all the networks and some stations operated.

Family Viewing Hour

I became the Code Review Board's senior member in the mid 1970s and dominated its deliberations for the next twenty years. The Code Review Board meetings in the 1970s were scenes of rancorous debates about the Family Viewing Hour.

The debacle over the Family Viewing Hour brought to a climax the debate on violence and sex on television. It also raised such questions as whether Federal Communications Commission (FCC) commissioner Richard Wiley with his jawboning to the networks was doing for the government what it could not do by regulation. Were his conversations more cajoling or did they have the weight of "state action" and a violation of the First Amendment? Was it to benefit the health and welfare of our children or the beginning of government control of programming?

Not just the broadcasters battled this major initiate to change television programming by creation of a "no violence and no sex" zone; the Hollywood production community also rose up in arms. They believed that their First Amendment rights were being trampled upon to their creative (and, of course, their economic) detriment. Norman Lear and Danny Arnold, among others, led the charge and brought suit to reverse the policy and also sought damages. A court ruling that eventually found the Family Viewing Hour unconstitutional was reversed on appeal, and the issue remains an open question.

The debate, however, over violence in television programs and the government's role in pushing for industry reform continues today.

As I looked at how I approached the portrayal of violence, the expression of love and sex, and the intertwining of the breaking of taboos in this three-decade review, I realized that television is a diary of our lives. Television programming is ultimately the culture. Family values have been in constant clash with the pushing of the envelope, the opening of reality, and the press of exploration.

The censor's role in television program review is delicate. If television indeed defines our culture as it both reports and sets the agenda, the censor is in a position to temper its message or permit an accurate reflection of its realities. A news editor has to determine how many times the Zapruder film of President John F. Kennedy's assassination should be run. How many times do we view excerpts of the beating of Rodney King? An entertainment editor has to determine how many programs can deal with child abuse or sexual harassment. How much violence is permissible? Should we show blood, decapitation, gore? Television acts out our conflicts and in doing so sometimes portrays our excesses. Television shows and applauds our sexuality while mirroring our behavior. How much skin do we show? Can two people— man and woman, man and man, woman and woman—be seen in bed together? Can they hold hands, can they "do it"?

Another major task of the censor involves the sensitive question of how to achieve balance. Unlike censors in other media, the television censor is the guardian of the public interest. The licensee, the owner or operator of a television station, owes his operating privilege to the public, but to run a successful business requires shareholder or private investment, advertiser support, and station distribution. Those dual realities, the government license and the economic enterprise nature of the business, put restraints on advocacy. The privilege carries the responsibility to preserve a sense of fairness and good taste in balancing diverse interests in the presentation of controversial issues. That is also the role of the gatekeeper.

The Television Docudrama

The docudrama is a form of drama/storytelling invented by the entertainment divisions of the networks to portray real people and real events. This type of drama is fraught with the danger of misleading the viewer. Its success, however, depends on dramatic moments of shock, sensation, jeopardy, fear, and personal grief. The censor finds himself constantly in the middle of satisfying these conflicting options.

Because of television's unique capability of visually bringing timely news and entertainment into the home, clear distinctions had to be made between fact and fiction. Dealing with a movie about Mae West, where legendary tales were not that harmful to the subject's public personae, was much different from presenting the life story of Jackie Kennedy Onassis. That docudrama, prepared without her cooperation, had to meticulously follow the public record for legal reasons as well as those of credibility.

In programs such as *Baby M*, the surrogate mother case, the court transcript became the bible. In *Separate but Equal*, based on the landmark case *Brown vs. Board of Education*, an irate and furious George Stevens Jr. battled, for dramatic license, for scenes that we felt were incorrect. Former president Richard Nixon never forgave ABC for telecasting "Final Days."

The telling of real events about real people constantly created battles, as truth and accuracy clashed with creative license for storytelling. To serve the public locally as a community station operator takes a great deal of discrimination and judgment. To serve the public from a network point of view can be accomplished only by consensus.

Responsibility, Respect, and Balance

The censor not only had the responsibility of being the conscience of the network and the arbiter of good taste, but he also had to answer to Congress on behalf of his company along with program and senior management.

The censor deals with certain givens. The medium is the message. The viewer believes what he sees, most of the time. Television's role is to entertain, to inform, to educate. Often it is difficult to distinguish one from the other. A license to broadcast is to operate in the public interest, convenience, and necessity. Often it is difficult to distinguish what is in the public interest and what is in the private, the advertiser, the advocates, or the creator's interest. So there is a censor—a gatekeeper.

"For better or for worse," Warren Burger, former chief justice of the Supreme Court, said,

> editing is what editors are for and editing is selection and choice of material. That editors—newspaper or broadcast— can and do abuse this power is beyond doubt, but that is not reason to deny the discretion [to the broadcaster] Congress provided. Calculated risks of abuse are taken in order to preserve higher values. The presence of these risks is nothing new, the authors of the Bill of Rights accepted the reality that these risks were evils for which there was no acceptable remedy other than a spirit of moderation and a sense of responsibility and civility on the part of those who exercise the guaranteed freedom of expression."

To act responsibly, to preserve a sense of fairness and good taste, to respect the dignity of man, to balance interests that the medium serves, to permit the exploration of new ideas and examination of old practices—these were some of my objectives as gatekeeper, censor, editor, and manager of change.

CENSORSHIP OF MUSIC AFTER THE SEPTEMBER 11 TERRORIST ATTACKS

Eric Nuzum

In the following selection, Eric Nuzum describes the climate of the music industry following the terrorist attacks of September 11, 2001. According to Nuzum, many people in the music industry felt that references to tall buildings, airplanes, or violence were inappropriate, and they therefore changed or suppressed song lyrics, album cover artwork, and music videos that might be considered offensive. However, the author explains, other musicians reported being pressured by the recording industry or government officials to self-censor their material. Nuzum also relates instances of censorship by radio stations, such as pulling controversial songs from their playlists. Nuzum is a music critic and the program director for Kent State University's public radio affiliate WKSU-FM in Ohio.

"Freedom has been attacked, but freedom will be defended."

These were the words of President George Bush shortly after the September 11th terrorist attacks on the United States. Bush went on to say that the terrorists "cannot touch the foundation of America" and "we go forward to defend freedom." Despite Bush's rhetoric, the actions of the U.S. government demonstrated a slightly different tact for protecting the American way of life. Within hours of the attacks, the Federal Bureau of Investigation (FBI) installed its controversial Carnivore system at some Internet providers to monitor and eavesdrop on electronic communications, especially those to and from accounts with Arabic names and words in the user IDs. Within two days, the U.S. Senate had adopted legislation making it easier for the FBI to obtain warrants. Also, within a week of the attacks, many elected representatives were promoting "anti-terrorism" legislation meant to allow law enforcement to gather private financial and education records and information, expand the definition of a "terrorist" to anyone who knows or should know that an organization they support in any way is a terrorist organization, and seize the property of those so suspected.

Eric Nuzum, "Crash into Me, Baby: America's Implicit Music Censorship in the Wake of September 11th," www.ericnuzum.com, September 29, 2002. Copyright © 2002 by Eric Nuzum. Reproduced by permission.

The words of other politicians didn't match those of their Commander in Chief. U.S. Senators Jon Kyl (R-Arizona) and Trent Lott (R-Mississippi), and House Democratic Leader Richard Gephardt (D-Missouri), all said that the erosion of civil liberties was "inevitable." "We're in a new world," Gephardt said. "We have to rebalance freedom and security." Vermont's governor, Howard Dean, said the crisis would require "a reevaluation of the importance of some of our specific civil liberties."

The American people seemed to get the message sent by their government: in order to protect you, you'll need to give up some of your freedom. The message resonated with the public, with an ABC–*Washington Post* poll finding 66% of Americans willing to give up some civil liberties to combat terrorism.

Further complicating the protection of civil rights in the United States was the myopic jingoism permeating America, creating an atmosphere of visceral intolerance. Peace activists and civil libertarians were branded as "un-American" and "crazy communists." Displays of American flags in public places became an expectation. One national talk show host referred to the American Civil Liberties Union as "the American version of al Qaida." Many unpopular and dissenting opinions were dismissed as "unpatriotic."

Changes to Lyrics and Videos

This put the American music industry in a difficult position. Traditionally a voice for almost all political and ideological persuasions, many artists and music companies felt the need to display some newfound sensitivity: Dave Matthews nixed plans to release "When the World Ends" as his next single, Bush changed the title of their new single from "Speed Kills" to "The People That We Love," the Cranberries pulled their video for "Analyse" because of its repeated images of skyscrapers and airplanes, Dream Theater changed the artwork from their three-disc live album to remove its renditions of burning New York buildings, and Sheryl Crow rewrote several lyrics for her upcoming album.

While many of these gestures were simple exercises in latent taste, others were not. For example, The Strokes removed the song "New York City Cops" from the U.S. version of their album *Is This It*. Like so many pop songs, the lyrics and theme of "New York City Cops" deal with a relationship, but it does contain some lyrics, such as "New York City cops—they ain't too smart," that could cause potential consternation in a post September 11th America.

The official Website for the group Rage Against the Machine—a high profile virtual soapbox and town square for social and political discussion and debate among the group's fans—shut down its discussion boards shortly after the attacks following queries to the band and site's management by federal officials. Further, the hip-hop group The

Coup was forced by their record label, 75 Ark, to change the artwork for their album *Party Music*. The original cover featured the group standing in front of an exploding World Trade Center. While admittedly eerie in the wake of the attacks, the artwork (originally created eighteen months earlier) bore no direct connection to the attacks. The cover had not been printed, but had been distributed electronically to media in anticipation of the album's release. Shortly after the attacks, the group's leader, Boots Riley, told *Wired.com* that the design "was supposed to be a metaphor for the capitalist state being destroyed through music." Though he had initially expressed concern about replacing the cover image, Riley backed down to pressure from his record company. "Two hours after the thing happened, we got the call saying, 'OK, you've got to have another album cover. No discussion,'" Riley remembers. "That was it. It was one of the first things that I saw in a series of censorship." The only further public comment on the cover came via a press statement released by the label which read, "75 Ark recognizes and supports the artistic freedom of its artists however, recent extraordinary events demand that we create new artwork for the album."

Sensitivities still remained high almost a year later. Steve Earle's song "John Walker Blues" [about the "American Taliban" fighter captured in Afghanistan by U.S. forces] ignited calls for its censorship in the *Wall Street Journal* and *The New York Post* two months before its release. The song looks at events through Walker's eyes, yet does not endorse Walker's actions or fate, nor does it take any ideological stance on Walker's beliefs. According to Nashville talk radio host Steve Gill, "Earle runs the risk of becoming the Jane Fonda of the war on terrorism by embracing John Walker and his Tali-buddies."

A List of Questionable Songs

However, the incident that received the most attention was a rumored list of songs banned from radio, each containing literal or metaphorical references a bit too close to recent events. The list, containing more than 150 songs described as "lyrically questionable," started as a grass-roots effort by local programmers, then was redistributed to all programmers by a senior executive at Clear Channel, the largest owner of radio stations in the United States. Among the listed songs were "Fly," "Jet Airliner," "Head Like a Hole," "Only the Good Die Young," "Great Balls of Fire," "Crash Into Me," "It's the End of the World as We Know It," and many more.

When the story hit the mainstream press, most journalists got the story wrong. In a series of lapsed journalistic judgments, reporters were too quick to believe that the list existed, then quick to believe it was a hoax.

It was widely reported that Clear Channel overtly banned the songs to avoid consternation and controversy, which wasn't true. The list did originate in several versions, circulated among colleagues at local radio stations. The lists were compiled by a senior vice president of programming at Clear Channel, and then e-mailed from corporate management to the more than 1,100 individual stations under Clear Channel's ownership. While the management e-mail did not call for an overt ban on songs, it did ask that programmers use "restraint" when selecting songs for airplay.

The story was initially reported on several radio industry web sites on September 14th, hitting the mainstream media on September 17th, led by a story on *Slate.com*. When the story spread through the media, Clear Channel released a cleverly worded press statement titled, "Clear Channel Says National 'Banned Playlist' Does Not Exist." In the release, the company stated, "Clear Channel Radio has not banned any songs from any of its radio stations." While the statement might seem to end the matter, the statement is just as telling for what it doesn't say as for what it does. Clear Channel correctly pointed out that the original e-mail didn't order anyone to ban any songs, but nowhere in the statement does the company deny that a list of "lyrically questionable" songs was created, edited by management, redistributed by management, and then acted upon by its employees. The statement denies the existence of an explicit ban, which is accurate, but does not deny the existence of the list. Further, the statement does not deny any censorious actions by its employees.

Explicit vs. Implicit Censorship

While Clear Channel is quick to point out there was no *explicit* censorship involved with the list, it is a perfect example of music censorship at its most *implicit*. Regardless of Clear Channel's intentions, censorship did occur. While many Clear Channel programmers were quoted in the media as saying that they did not follow the suggestions of the e-mail, many times more said they did indeed remove songs from broadcast because of the list or its suggested sense of restraint.

Unfortunately, the media didn't apply the necessary scrutiny to Clear Channel's statement. Just as quickly as the media was swept into the controversy, the entire incident was written off as a "hoax," disappearing from public discussion. Thanks to Clear Channel's savvy statement, the company had convinced the press that the list didn't exist at all; that earlier reports were no more credible than any other Internet hoax, such as get rich quick chain e-mail schemes or tales of sick children needing correspondence.

Arguments over the complicated truth of various accusations and denials surrounding the Clear Channel list tend to distort the most troubling aspects of the incident. The real issue lies in the list's content, leading one to wonder exactly what Clear Channel's executives and programmers were trying to restrain.

While the list was mainly comprised of songs bearing lyrical references to burning, death, and airplanes, it also advocated censure for "Peace Train" by Cat Stevens, John Lennon's "Imagine," and all songs by Rage Against the Machine. What do these songs have to do with flying airplanes into buildings? Absolutely nothing. Yet in the past each of these artists has expressed controversial political sentiments that buck against mainstream beliefs.

"If our songs are 'questionable' in any way, it is that they encourage people to question the kind of ignorance that breeds intolerance," said Rage Against the Machine's Tom Morello in an e-mail statement. "Intolerance which can lead to censorship and the extinguishing of our civil liberties, or at its extremes can lead to the kind of violence we witnessed."

The inclusion of many of the list's songs shows a troubling degree of literalism and prejudice when examining lyrical imagery. For example, "I Go to Pieces" was one of two songs by Peter and Gordon included on the list. "I suppose a song about someone going to pieces could be upsetting if someone took it literally," said the group's Peter Asher. "But 'I can't live without love' is a sentiment that's as true in crisis as it is in normal times. It's a totally pro-love sentiment and could only be helpful right now."

A Slippery Slope

The list's existence and resulting actions are a perfect example of how a well-intentioned attempt at "sensitivity" can quickly careen down the slippery slope towards stifled free expression. This is hardly the first time American radio has taken such well-intentioned, yet censorious, action.

Back in 1940, the NBC radio network banned 147 popular songs containing potential sexual innuendo, including Billie Holiday's version of "Love for Sale," calling these songs "obscene." In 1942, the United States government sent radio broadcasters a list of wartime practices, including a ban on weather forecasts (which might help enemies plan air attacks), and a suspension of listener requests (fearing it might allow the transmission of coded messages). In order to safeguard the morality of America's youth, *Billboard* Magazine got behind a 1954 effort to rid radio of black R&B artists, claiming they "show bad taste and a disregard for recognized moral standards." In 1967, the ABC radio network and a group called the American Mothers' Committee tried to remove all songs from airplay that "glorify sex, blasphemy, and drugs." In 1970, the Federal Communications Commission—under pressure from the Nixon administration and working with a list of songs compiled by the U.S. Army—sent a telegram to all radio owners warning them to remove all songs condoning drug use. Their list of songs included "Yellow Submarine," "Eight Miles High," and "Puff (The Magic Dragon)."

The idea of what was considered offensive or dangerous may have been different back then, but the reason such censorship needs to be resisted is the same. When we open the question of "tasteful" or "appropriate" censorship—even a little—we turn rights into permissions. This month, radio might not want to offend those affected by tragedy or jeopardize domestic security; next time they may not want to play music that criticizes the government. You can imagine where this ends up.

Defending Artistic Freedom

Unfortunately, defending music is easily dismissed by some Americans as comparatively trivial in the wake of these horrible and gruesome tragedies. But should artistic liberties be cast aside in a time of national crisis? That depends on what you define as freedom. Music's reach and pervasiveness puts it on the cutting edge of that definition.

Defense of artistic rights is a multifarious example of the importance of protecting civil liberties—even on their periphery. While electronic wiretapping and the boundaries of search-and-seizure laws may not excite or directly impact a large number of Americans, their ability to hear "Stairway to Heaven" or "Lucy in the Sky with Diamonds" does.

In America, we are exposed to more music in a day than any other art form, perhaps more than all other forms of art combined. We use music in the most significant and most mundane of our activities, both to focus intense feelings and to distract us from the occasional dullness of life. While censors justify their actions based on music's suggested *provocative* potential, their actions completely disregard music's demonstrated *evocative* nature. Thus, as we impede music, we inhibit our ability to be fully human.

Music doesn't have to be patriotic, sensitive, or even make sense. Music, at its most fundamental core, *is* freedom.

It just needs to be there.

THE GOVERNMENT SHOULD LIMIT FREE SPEECH IN THE MEDIA

Robert Peters

In the following selection, Robert Peters declares that it is morally wrong for the media to expose children to graphic violence and lewd sexual images. The First Amendment was not intended to allow the news and entertainment industries to depict extremely violent or sexual scenes that have no social value, he argues. Since sensational material often garners high ratings, he maintains, it is unlikely that the media will practice self-censorship. Therefore, Peters advocates government regulation of news and entertainment programming. Peters is the president of Morality in Media, a national interfaith organization headquartered in New York that monitors violence and pornography in the media.

I was born in 1949. Not all was well in the U.S. at that time, but if we compare the rates in the 1950s of teen abortion, premarital sex, sexually transmitted diseases, unwed pregnancies and births, and violent crime, with the rates in the 1990s, we discover that the rates for teens have skyrocketed.

Searching for the Cause

Clearly, no one cause explains the rise. Since the 1950s there has been a breakdown of authority in the home and public schools. The positive influence of religion has declined. There has been a dramatic increase in use of illegal drugs. The tragic cycle of poverty has taken its toll, as has mental illness.

But it is parents, religious institutions, schools, peers and popular culture that are the primary sources of role models and values for youth. Parents, schools and religious institutions certainly have changed since the 1950s, but few are telling kids it is OK to engage in promiscuous sex and violent crime.

Peers haven't changed much either. They've always been a bad influence! What has changed drastically in the last 30–40 years has been the content of "popular culture." It is, to shocking degree, more vulgar, more sexual and more violent.

To blame all sexual misbehavior and violent crime on the media would, of course, be absurd, but to say that there is absolutely no causal relationship whatsoever between sex and violence in the media and misbehavior in real life would be equally absurd.

When common sense, personal experience, piles of anecdotal evidence and a substantial body of social science research all point to some sort of causal relationship, the burden of proof should shift to those who say there is no connection.

The Nature of Media Responsibility

There are two levels of media responsibility: moral and legal. As defined in *Webster's New World Dictionary* (3rd College Edition, 1988), "moral" means: "relating to, dealing with, or capable of making the distinction between, right and wrong in conduct".

As I see it, it is wrong for "Hollywood" to churn out films that depict in graphic and often sadistic detail, exploitative deadly violence that is imitable, even by children.

It is wrong for broadcast TV networks to churn out programming that is vulgar and lewd and that provides endless "role models" for sexual promiscuity, adultery and perversion.

It is wrong for cable and satellite TV operators to provide cable versions of hardcore porn films on a pay-per-view basis.

It is wrong for radio stations to broadcast explicit rap lyrics that boast about rape and other sexual abuse of women or to broadcast the gutter talk of "shock jocks" such as Howard Stern.

It is wrong for media news departments to milk almost every sex scandal and horrific crime that comes along for every ratings point that can be extracted from it. Preoccupation with stories that are attention grabbing but which do not inform or educate about important public issues does not serve the public interest. News stories can also beget copycat behavior.

The Scope of the First Amendment

Misconceptions about the First Amendment notwithstanding, there are also legal responsibilities. As Justice Brennan put it in *Roth v. United States*, (1957):

> "[I]t is apparent that the unconditional phrasing of the First Amendment was not intended to protect every utterance."

Among the various laws that could impact the manner in which sex or violence is portrayed in the media are those governing:

• Aiding and abetting a crime
• Inciting unlawful conduct
• Indecency
• Invasion of privacy

- Obscenity
- Porn Victims' Compensation Act (Illinois)
- Sexual exploitation of a child

Two issues that have generated a great deal of discussion in recent years are whether the First Amendment (1) prevents government from regulating media violence to protect children or (2) prevents persons from suing the media for harms suffered because of the irresponsible manner in which violence is depicted.

I do not think the First Amendment prevents government from restricting minors' access to entertainment that glamorizes violence causing serious bodily injury or death, no matter how exploitative, gratuitous, graphic and easily imitable it is.

I recognize that drawing lines between speech protected by the First Amendment and speech that is not can present difficulties. But if the Supreme Court, in order to protect adults on the job, can identify forms of "sexual expression" that constitute illegal sexual harassment, the Court, in order to protect children, can also identify forms of media violence that cannot legally be shown to children, at least in the absence of a parent or guardian.

I would add that commercial portrayals of hardcore violence as entertainment and for no other reason than to make a profit, surely lie at the periphery of First Amendment concern.

I also do not think the First Amendment was intended to shield the media from all responsibility for any and all harms resulting from irresponsible portrayals of violence. In discussing the extent of freedom of the press, the Supreme Court said in *Near v. Minnesota*, (1931):

> [T]he main purpose of such provisions is "to prevent all such previous restraints upon publications as had been practiced by other governments". . . . [T]hey do not prevent *subsequent punishment of such as may be deeemed contrary to the public welfare.* . . . The point of criticism has been "that . . . the liberty of the press might be rendered a mockery . . . if while every man was at liberty to publish what he pleased, the public authorities might nevertheless punish him for *harmless* publications.". . . *But it is recognized that punishment for the abuse of the liberty accorded to the press is essential to the protection of the public*, and that the common law rules that subject the libeler to *responsibility* for the public offense, as well as the private injury, are not abolished by the protection extended in our constitutions. [Emphasis added]

The *Near* case focused on libelous material, but in *Chaplinsky v. New Hampshire*, (1942), the Court elaborated on the scope of First Amendment protection:

> There are certain well-defined and narrowly limited classes of speech, the prevention and punishment of which have never

been thought to raise any Constitutional problem. These include the lewd and obscene, the profane, the libelous, and the insulting or "fighting" words—those which by their very utterance inflict injury. . . . It has been well observed that such utterances are no essential part of any exposition of ideas, and are of such slight social value as a step to truth that any benefit that may be derived from them is clearly outweighed by the social interest in order and morality.

While some depictions of media violence (e.g., the slaughter in *Private Ryan* and *Schindler's List*) are undoubtedly intended to be part of an "exposition of ideas," it is all too clear to any honest observer that much if not most media violence is exploitative, unnecessary and of no "social value."

In saying that I do not think the First Amendment should shield the media from all responsibility for harms resulting from irresponsible portrayals of violence, I do not say the media should be strictly liable. Looking again to libel law, persons who make false defamatory statements can be held liable only if they acted with a lack of care amounting to at least negligence. In some cases involving media, actual malice must be proved.

Furthermore, the law of negligence often aims more at reducing or minimizing risks rather than eliminating them. No matter how responsibly an act of violence is portrayed in the media, there is always a risk that someone could get a "wrong idea" and act on it. Most experts on media violence are not saying that the media should never portray a violent act. They are saying that the manner in which media violence is portrayed can decrease the risks of harm.

Living in a "Democratic Society"

The First Amendment speaks first about the free exercise of religion and then about freedom of speech and of the press. No one argues that the "free exercise" clause guarantees to every American the right to do or say anything, as long as it is motivated by sincere or, perhaps, semi-sincere religious belief.

One well known civil libertarian organization, however, does argue that the First Amendment protects *all* "sexual expression," including child pornography. Civil libertarians are now rising to the defense of "violent expression" with much the same vigor and absolutism that propelled their misguided defense of pornography.

I think the Supreme Court got it right when it rejected the extreme view that First Amendment protection for speech and press is absolute. I think the Court got it right when it recognized that the First Amendment would often require finding a balance between legitimate societal interests and personal freedoms.

I think the majority of Americans are rightly concerned about the effect that media sex and violence is having on society in general and youth in particular. I think they want something done about it—and if the media won't do it, then government should.

But in a "democratic society" such as ours, some compromises may also be necessary. For example, while it may be acceptable for consenting adults to choose to view a particular film or TV program depicting sex or violence, it will often not be acceptable to distribute it to minors or in a manner or in a medium that makes it difficult, if not impossible, for unconsenting adults to avoid. For example, there is a difference between a premium cable TV channel, like HBO, and a basic cable or broadcast TV channel.

There is an old saying, "Your rights end where mine begin." There is a basic human right enjoyed by all Americans, young and old, to live in a safe, healthy and decent society. At present, much of "popular culture" is at war with that right. The media could correct the problems without government intervention, but it is doubtful whether the media will accept the responsibility.

THE MEDIA SHOULD PRACTICE SELF-REGULATION

The Federal Trade Commission

The Federal Trade Commission (FTC) is the government agency charged with promoting free-market competition and monitoring unfair trade practices. In the report that follows, the FTC contends that the media and entertainment industries routinely market motion pictures, music recordings, and electronic games with violent content to children under seventeen years of age. Rather than impose government censorship that would violate First Amendment protections, the FTC recommends instead that the media and entertainment industries practice self-regulation. The commission suggests several measures, including establishing codes that prohibit the marketing of violent products to children, preventing those products from being sold to children, and educating parents about ratings and labels that describe violent content.

On September 11, 2000, the Federal Trade Commission (FTC) released its report titled "Marketing Violent Entertainment to Children: A Review of Self-Regulation and Industry Practices in the Motion Picture, Music Recording & Electronic Game Industries." The report was conducted in response to a request from President Bill Clinton on June 1, 1999, as well as similar requests from members of Congress, to answer two questions about the marketing of violent entertainment material: Do the industries promote products they themselves acknowledge warrant parental caution in venues where children make up a substantial percentage of the audience? And are these advertisements intended to attract children and teenagers? The report found that "for all three segments of the entertainment industry, the answers are plainly 'yes.'"

The report finds that while the entertainment industry has taken steps to identify content that may not be appropriate for children, the companies in those industries still routinely target children under 17 in their marketing of products their own ratings systems deem inappropriate or warrant parental caution due to violent content. The FTC found evidence of marketing and media plans that expressly target

The Federal Trade Commission, "FTC Releases Report on the Marketing of Violent Entertainment to Children," www.ftc.gov, September 11, 2000.

children under 17, and promote and advertise products in media out-
lets most likely to reach children under 17. The report also publishes
an FTC survey that shows children under 17 are frequently able to
buy tickets to R-rated movies without parental accompaniment and
purchase music recordings and electronic games with parental advisory labels or that are restricted to an older audience.

In response to these findings, the Commission recommends additional action by the industry to enhance their self-regulatory efforts.
The report makes no legislative recommendations to Congress on this
issue.

According to FTC Chairman Robert Pitofsky, the report illustrates
clear shortcomings in industry efforts to limit access to age-inappropriate
material to children. "Companies in the entertainment industry routinely undercut their own rating restrictions by target marketing violent
films, records, and video games to young audiences. These industries
can and should do better than this report illustrates."

Key Findings

The report makes the following key findings about the marketing of
violent entertainment material by the industry:

Movies: Of the 44 movies rated R for violence the Commission
selected for its study, the Commission found that 35, or 80 percent,
were targeted to children under 17. Marketing plans for 28 of those
44, or 64 percent, contained express statements that the films target
audience included children under 17. Plans for the other seven
movies were either extremely similar to the plans of the films that did
identify an under-17 target audience, or they detailed plans indicating
they were targeting that age group, such as promoting the film in
high schools or publications with majority under-17 audiences.

Music: Of the 55 music recordings with explicit content labels the
Commission selected for its review, the Commission found that all
were targeted to children under 17. Marketing plans for 15, or 27 percent, expressly identified children under 17 as part of their target
audience. The documents for the remaining 40 explicit-content
labeled recordings did not expressly state the age of the target audience, but detailed plans indicating they were targeting that age group,
including placing advertising in media that would reach a majority or
substantial percentage of children under 17.

Games: Of the 118 electronic games with a Mature rating for violence, the Commission selected for its study, 83, or 70 percent, targeted children under 17. The marketing plans for 60 of these, or 51
percent, expressly included children under 17 in the target audience.
Documents for the remaining 23 games showed plans to advertise in
magazines or on television shows with a majority or substantial
under-17 audience.

In addition to the information gathered on marketing, the FTC conducted studies from May–July 2000 on children's ability to buy violent entertainment material, which found most retailers make little effort to restrict children's access to products with violent content. Just under half the movie theaters admitted children ages 13 to 16 to R-rated films even when not accompanied by an adult. The surveys also revealed that unaccompanied children ages 13 to 16 were able to buy both explicit recordings and Mature-rated electronic games 85 percent of the time.

Recommendations

Self-regulation is especially critical in this area, given the First Amendment protections that prohibit government regulation of these products' content. While the industries reviewed have taken positive steps to address some of these concerns, the Commission believes that all three industries should do more to enhance their self-regulatory efforts. The industry should:

Establish or expand codes that prohibit target marketing to children and impose sanctions for violations. All three industries should improve the usefulness of their ratings and labels by establishing codes that prohibit marketing R-rated/M-rated/explicit-labeled products in media or venues with a substantial under-17 audience. In addition, the Commission suggests that each industry's trade associations monitor and encourage their members' compliance with these policies and impose meaningful sanctions for non-compliance.

Increase compliance at the retail level by checking identification or requiring parental permission before selling tickets to R movies, and by not selling or renting products labeled "Explicit" or rated R or M, to children under 17.

Increase parental understanding of the ratings and labels by including the reasons for the rating or the label in all advertising and product packaging. The Commission also calls on the industry to continue efforts to educate parents—and children—about the meanings of ratings and descriptors.

According to the Commission, implementation of these suggestions would significantly improve the present self-regulatory regimes: "Self-regulatory programs can work only if the concerned industry associations monitor compliance and ensure that violations have consequences." In addition, the Commission believes that "continuous public oversight is also required and that Congress should continue to monitor the progress of self-regulation in this area."

MEDIA CENSORSHIP VIOLATES THE RIGHT TO FREE SPEECH

Free Expression Policy Project

In the following selection, the Free Expression Policy Project (FEPP) argues that censoring violent images and controversial ideas in the media is a violation of the First Amendment and a poor substitute for seriously addressing concerns about disagreeable media messages. Furthermore, the FEPP maintains, it is impossible to draw any conclusive evidence about the effects of media violence from experiments and studies. As an alternative to censorship, the FEPP advocates what it considers more effective solutions, including media literacy education and increased support for nonviolent television programming. Based in New York, the FEPP supports artistic and intellectual freedom by providing empirical research, policy development, and other useful resources for anti-censorship advocacy.

This selection answers some frequently-asked questions about social science research into the effects of media violence. The bottom line is that despite the claims of some psychologists and politicians, the actual research results have been weak and ambiguous.

This should not be surprising: media violence is so pervasive in our lives, and comes in so many different contexts and styles, that it is impossible to make accurate generalizations about its real-world effects based on experiments in a laboratory, or on studies that simply find statistical correlations between media viewing and aggressive behavior.

Of course, the First Amendment would be a significant barrier to censoring violent images and ideas even if social science had in fact produced statistical evidence of adverse effects. But it is important for the ongoing debate on this issue that the real facts about media violence studies are understood.

Flawed Research

No one seriously doubts that the mass media have profound effects on our attitudes and behavior. But the effects vary tremendously, depending on the different ways that media content is presented, and the personality, background, intelligence, and life experience of the viewer.

Although many people believe that media violence causes aggression, it's doubtful that this can ever be proved by the methods of social science. For one thing, violent images and ideas come in too many different styles and contexts for researchers to be able to make meaningful generalizations about effects.

Somewhere between 200 and 300 laboratory experiments, field studies, and correlational studies have been done on media violence (not thousands, as some activists have claimed), and their results are dubious and inconsistent. In some cases, experimenters have manipulated disappointing results until they came up with at least one positive finding; then proclaimed that the experiment supported their hypothesis that media violence causes aggression. Some experiments have found more aggressive behavior after viewing nonviolent shows like *Sesame Street* and *Mr. Rogers' Neighborhood.*

Professor Jonathan Freedman of the University of Toronto, an independent expert who reviewed the media violence literature in the 1980s, concluded that the research did not "provide either strong or consistent support for the hypothesis that exposure to media violence causes aggression or crime. Rather, the results have been extremely inconsistent and weak." Updating his research in 2002, Freedman reported that fewer than half the studies support a causal effect.

For the minority of experiments that have yielded positive results, the explanation probably has more to do with the general arousal effect of violent entertainment than with viewers actually imitating violent acts. Laboratory experiments, moreover, do not measure real aggression but other behaviors that the researchers consider "proxies" for real aggression—popping balloons, giving noise blasts, hitting Bobo dolls, or other forms of aggressive play.

Laboratory experiments also suffer from "experimenter demand effect"—subjects responding to what they think the researcher wants. They know that behavior is permitted in the lab that would be unacceptable in the real world.

Because of the weakness of laboratory experiments in predicting behavior, psychologists have undertaken "field experiments" that more accurately replicate the real world. Freedman reported that the overwhelming majority of field experiments found no adverse effects on behavior from exposure to media violence.

Some correlational studies show a "link" or "association" between the subjects' amount of violent TV viewing and real-world aggressive behavior. But a link or association does not establish causation. It is likely that a combination of factors (level of intelligence, education, social background and attitudes, genetic predisposition, and economic status) account for both the entertainment preferences and the behavior.

Some correlational studies do not even focus on violent TV but simply examine overall amount of television viewing. This reinforces the probability that people whose cultural and activity choices are limited and who thus watch excessive amounts of TV also may have a more limited range of responses to conflict situations.

Different Reactions by Different Viewers

Violence has been a subject in literature and the arts since the beginning of human civilization. In part, this simply reflects the unfortunate realities of the world. But it's also likely that our fascination with violence satisfies some basic human needs. The adrenaline rush, the satisfaction of imagination, fantasy, and vicarious adventure, probably explain why millions of nonviolent people enjoy violent entertainment.

Because the mass media presents violence in so many different ways (news, sports, action movies, cartoons, horror movies, documentaries, war stories with pacifist themes), it is particularly difficult to generalize about its impact. Even social scientists who believe that violent entertainment has adverse effects don't agree on what kinds of violent images or ideas are harmful. Some point to cartoons; others point to movies in which a violent hero is rewarded; others fault the gory focus of television news.

There have been instances where criminals or others engaged in violent behavior have imitated specific aspects of a violent movie or TV show. But the fact that millions of other viewers have not engaged in imitation suggests that predisposition is the important factor, and that if the bad actors had not seen that particular movie or show, they would have imitated something else. It is impossible to predict which episodes or descriptions will be imitated by unstable individuals, and equally impossible to ban every book, movie, magazine article, song, game, or other cultural product that somebody might imitate.

There is much that is pernicious, banal, and crude in popular culture—not all of it violent. The best ways to address concerns about bad media messages of all types are media literacy education and increased funding for creative, educational, nonviolent TV programming.

Reprinted with permission from the Free Expression Policy Project, www. fepproject.org, footnotes omitted. For footnotes and sources, go to fepproject. org/factsheets/mediaviolence.html.

CHAPTER 3

INTERNET CENSORSHIP

AN OVERVIEW OF LEGISLATION REGARDING INTERNET PORNOGRAPHY

Jason Krause

In the article that follows, Jason Krause examines the history of legislative efforts to ban pornography on the Internet. According to Krause, many legislators and citizens are worried about the dangers of exposing children to pornographic material on the Internet. Starting in the mid-1990s, he explains, the U.S. Congress has passed several acts designed to protect children from Internet obscenity. However, the author writes, these acts have been criticized by civil libertarians for violating free speech, and the U.S. Supreme Court has often ruled them unconstitutional. He also explores the difficulties involved in relying on pre-Internet anti-obscenity legal precedents to argue cases for censorship in the new electronic medium. Krause is a legal affairs writer for the *ABA Journal*, a monthly magazine published by the American Bar Association.

As best as anyone involved can remember, the war on Internet pornography started in earnest on June 5, 1995, the day then–U.S. Sen. James Exon's blue book first showed up on Capitol Hill.

The blue book, actually a blue binder, was originally brought to the Hill by anti-obscenity activists trying to bring attention to their cause and included descriptions of pornographic material freely available on the Web. Later, someone added hardcore pornographic pictures downloaded from online newsgroups to illustrate the book.

The blue book was never entered into the Congressional Record, but after Exon, a Nebraska Democrat, started passing it around the Senate it became a catalyst for bipartisan support of anti-porn legislation for the Internet. For several years, Exon had waged a lonely fight to inspire interest in his bill to protect children from indecent material on the then-nascent Net. But after he started passing around the blue binder, the Senate developed a mighty case of righteous indignation at Internet obscenity.

"Before we had the blue book, no one wanted to hear anything about obscenity and the Internet," says Donna Rice Hughes, an

Jason Krause, "Can Anyone Stop Internet Porn?" *ABA Journal*, September 2002.

activist whose organization, Enough Is Enough, originally compiled the book. "But as soon as they started reading about what was going on in newsgroups, we were suddenly able to pass the bill. And we did it by an overwhelming margin after only two or three days of debate."

Indeed, in 1996 the bill that became the Communications Decency Act (CDA) passed the Senate by a vote of 91–5 and later sailed through the House 414–16. The CDA made it a crime simply to put adult-oriented material online where children can find it.

Yet early on there were rumblings that Congress may have overreacted. House Speaker Newt Gingrich worried that "it is clearly a violation of free speech and it is a violation of the rights of adults to communicate with each other."

A year later, the U.S. Supreme Court struck down the CDA as unconstitutional in *ACLU v. Reno*. Writing for the court, Justice John Paul Stevens called the CDA "wholly unprecedented" in its breadth and a "content-based blanket restriction on speech."

Since then, Congress has passed three more major pieces of Internet porn legislation. One has been struck down and the other two are in limbo:

- The 1996 Child Pornography Prevention Act (CPPA), which banned computer-generated pornographic images of children. In April 2002, the U.S. Supreme Court shot down provisions of the CPPA outlawing those virtual depictions.
- The 1998 Child Online Protection Act (COPA), Congress's attempt to replace the Communications Decency Act. COPA required commercial Web sites to collect a credit card number or other proof of age before allowing Internet users to view material deemed harmful to minors. In May 2002 the Supreme Court sent the case back to the 3rd U.S. Circuit Court of Appeals at Philadelphia for further review.
- The 2000 Children's Internet Protection Act (CIPA) required public libraries to use filters on their computers or risk losing federal funding. In May 2002 a federal district court in Philadelphia found CIPA unconstitutional because it would inevitably restrict access for adults to protected speech. In June 2002 the Department of Justice filed a petition for certiorari [further review] with the Supreme Court.

Fighting Internet Porn

So far, the anti-obscenity forces have little to show for all their efforts in Congress. Meanwhile, Internet pornography has become an inescapable fact and a big business.

Yet Internet obscenity law proponents persist. "The courts have said again and again that we are not wrong in our intentions," says David Crane, who has co-authored every piece of child protection law to pass Congress so far. "It's just our methods that needed work."

Indeed, if there is one man who has been at the center of the legislation it is Crane, a 37-year-old senior vice president with the D.C.-based lobbying firm The Washington Group. As a legislative assistant, Crane worked with senators and anti-porn advocates in drafting the legislation. He continues to help draft similar legislation as a consultant.

Crane got involved in Internet anti-porn law as a legislative assistant for Sens. Dan Coates, R-Ind., and later John McCain, R-Ariz. He drafted the bill that became the CDA when Republican Coates joined Democrat Exon in crafting a bipartisan Internet porn bill. Since then, Crane has made Internet child-porn legislation a specialty.

As a lobbyist, Crane now works out of a corner office with a view of the city. Though mild mannered, he becomes animated when the subject turns to his specialty. From his point of view, the forces that have opposed these bills—groups like the American Civil Liberties Union (ACLU) and Internet publishers such as Salon.com—have unfairly attacked the laws. The anti-obscenity bills don't in any way inhibit legitimate, protected speech on the Net, Crane says.

"Everyone acts like the Internet is this pristine environment that should be free from regulation," says Crane. "But Congress has written these bills to be narrow enough that people like Salon should have nothing to worry about. They don't seem to realize there's a big difference between being a libertarian and a libertine."

Fighting Internet Censorship

Of course, not everyone is convinced the anti-obscenity forces in Congress can or even want to write a narrow enough law that can protect both children and Internet speech at the same time.

"Some argue, and I am among them, that there is no way to do it right. The First Amendment limits have been set and the Supreme Court will enforce [those limits] every time," says Ann Beeson, the ACLU attorney who argued the COPA case before the Supreme Court. "There is no doubt in my mind the real agenda is not so much to protect children but to prevent adults from viewing indecent materials."

So far, courts seem to have adopted Beeson's viewpoint. The sticking point is how—indeed whether—the Internet is suited to the same kinds of obscenity laws that have passed muster in the real world.

"There are laws to protect minors from indecency in the real world, but we don't have any such laws online," says Rice Hughes. "What we want is to put a virtual cellophane wrapper on the Internet."

But will a cellophane wrapper fit something as expansive and unwieldy as the Internet? The problem with porn laws traditionally has been balancing the rights of adults to view protected materials with the government's interest in prosecuting obscenity, which lacks First Amendment protection. The Supreme Court historically has affirmed the government's interest in protecting children from obscenity. But as yet, not one of these Internet porn laws has managed to balance that interest and protect free speech for adults, at least in a final review by the Supreme Court.

For example, a shortcoming of the CDA was use of the vague, undefined terms "indecent" and "patently offensive." The statute would have criminalized material protected for adults. That's because *Ginsberg v. New York* (1968), the case that defined the term "harmful to minors," insisted that "only in relatively narrow and well-defined circumstances may government bar public dissemination of protected material" to children.

Adapting Anti-Pornography Legislation

So after the CDA's rebuke in *Reno*, the anti-obscenity forces took a new tack in drafting legislation. Congress drafted separate, narrower bills to address piecemeal the same concerns as did the CDA: one measure to regulate pornography in libraries (CIPA), one to address pornographic Web sites (COPA), and one to address computer-generated child porn (CPPA).

"We had to negotiate a bit with ourselves, but basically what we do is see what the court accepts and what it rejects and adjust accordingly," says Crane. "In writing COPA, essentially what we did is we took *Reno* and narrowed our approach. We switched from a shotgun to a rifle and tried to tailor it precisely to the courts' demands."

Indeed, in the summer of 2002 the House passed the Child Obscenity and Pornography Prevention Act. COPPA is a response to the Supreme Court's earlier rejection in *Ashcroft v. Free Speech Coalition* of the Child Pornography Prevention Act's virtual depiction ban. Among other provisions, the new bill would strengthen a defendant's affirmative defense that the Internet images were not those of actual children.

And, according to Rice Hughes and others, a Senate bill is in the works to stop pornographic spam e-mails from reaching children.

However, there is a risk that these new bills might be written so narrowly as to be practically useless. "Congress took a punch in the nose with the last virtual child porn bill [CPPA], and they're accepting the knockdown," says Bruce Taylor, an anti-obscenity activist with the National Law Center in Fairfax, Va. Taylor, a former federal prosecutor who co-authored the legislation with Crane, calls COPPA "so weak that what it actually does is effectively legalize child computer porn."

But the anti-obscenity forces may have a more fundamental problem: No matter how narrow, the reactive legislation nevertheless falls apart when it enters the world of cyberspace. When it comes to the Internet, the rules that traditionally govern the real world often become distorted.

Take, for example, the COPA case, now back in the 3rd Circuit. To rectify the CDA's shortcomings, changes were worked into COPA to narrow the bill so it would not restrict Internet free speech. The statute would apply to material displayed only on the World Wide Web, the portion of the Internet where most commercial sites are found; it would cover only communications made for commercial purposes; and it would restrict only material that is harmful to minors.

And this time around, COPA clearly defined what is harmful to minors by appropriating the language of the three-part obscenity test set forth in *Miller v. California* (1973), the touchstone case for determining obscenity. The test asks whether the average person applying contemporary community standards would find that a work appeals to a prurient interest; whether a work depicts sexual conduct specifically defined by the applicable law; and whether the work, taken as a whole, lacks serious literary, artistic, political or scientific value.

The Community Standards Problem

However, the unintended consequence of relying on the *Miller* test was to force the courts to wrestle with the fundamental question of whether the community standards test applied to the Internet, with its global reach. How, for example, do you define a community with no geographic borders?

That, essentially, is what the 3rd Circuit asked when it upheld a district court injunction barring enforcement of the statute. Though Beeson and the ACLU raised the question of community standards on the Internet in their briefs, most observers agree that the 3rd Circuit threw everyone a curve when it raised the issue.

"We had a lot of discussions about fighting COPA on community standards grounds, and the argument was probably in most early drafts of various amicus briefs," says Washington, D.C., attorney Robert Corn-Revere, a First Amendment lawyer. "But I think everyone decided it would be much easier to argue the case without raising the question of community standards. It was too thorny."

The question also stymied the Supreme Court when it heard *Ashcroft v. ACLU*. In their decision, Justices Anthony M. Kennedy, Sandra Day O'Connor, Stephen G. Breyer, David Souter and Ruth Bader Ginsburg either concurred or joined other justices in writing one of three separate opinions wrestling with how to reconcile the community standards test with the Internet. The only thing all the justices agreed on was to remand the decision to the 3rd Circuit.

However, not all the justices were so troubled. Justice Clarence Thomas, writing the court's opinion, seemed to have little patience with any claims for the Internet's exceptionality as a communications medium. In fact, he recommended that if a publisher cannot comply with COPA's community standards test, then it should simply get off the Net.

"If a publisher wishes for its material to be judged only by the standards of particular communities, it need only take the simple step of utilizing a medium that enables it to target the release of its material into those communities," Thomas wrote.

Though the court ultimately took a pass at reinterpreting the test this time, it is probably inevitable that the question will come back. "Someday, someone in Alabama will try to prosecute a Web site operator in New York, and that's going to upset everything," says Beeson.

While there is discord among the justices over defining community standards for the Net, no one is willing to say that the *Miller* test is unusable or needs to be tossed out. There is, however, a growing consensus that it needs to be reworked to account for the Internet.

"I wouldn't say it's broken, but it is in tension," says Corn-Revere. "I'm not sure anyone knows how to repair it right now."

Such arguments are particularly frustrating to many anti-porn activists, who complain the arguments come from people who have nothing to fear from this legislation.

"No one who sued [over] COPA should have had standing. Notice how none of them were the pornographers [the bill] was really aimed at," says Taylor. "Of course, the ACLU asks the court to read these laws as broadly as possible, and the court followed that lead and read it so broadly so as to include protected speech."

But among COPA's detractors, Web publishers such as San Francisco–based Salon say that the statute and other Internet anti-obscenity laws are still too broad and would impose impossible financial burdens.

"Salon does not address minors or market to minors; we're very clear that we are aimed at grownups," says Salon managing editor Scott Rosenberg. "But if we had to verify that every single person who tried to access our site was a grownup by demanding credit card numbers from them, it would strangle our business."

Opponents also complain that many of the changes Congress made are merely cosmetic and fail to address the fundamental flaws in the legislation that made it overbroad. For example, says Corn-Revere, when the CPPA was struck down, "The court took issue with the language that referred to material that 'appears to be a child.' So when Congress rewrote the law it modified the language to read 'virtually indistinguishable' from a child. I mean, get real. I fail to see how that kind of change is responsive or flexible at all."

Continuing the Controversy

But with continued support in Congress for Internet anti-obscenity laws, more of these bills will certainly be passed. Every time one child-protection law is turned down, the authors try to write a new bill that addresses the court's problems with the last. "If the courts do manage to reject [COPA], all it means is that [Congress must] tailor a new law to the decision," says Crane.

One lesson the anti-obscenity law authors have learned is that Internet porn legislation must be written very explicitly, or the courts will assume the worst about Congress' intentions. For example, Taylor says the Supreme Court's recent debate over community standards could have been avoided if the justices had only read Congress' committee reports on COPA. "If they'd read the House committee report, they'd see Congress specifically recommended a nongeographic, age-based standard to determine what adults think is harmful to minors," says Taylor. "The lesson we've learned is that Congress should put the same explicit language that's found in committee reports into the bill because apparently we can't just assume that the courts read the reports anymore."

And there is an important new ally in the fight against Internet obscenity who may finally force the issue: Attorney General John Ashcroft. In June 2002, the Department of Justice held a symposium at the National Advocacy Center, a modern facility for training U.S. attorneys in Columbia, S.C.

The crowd included veteran prosecutors of wars against pornography from the 1980s and '90s, and members of U.S. attorneys' offices. Ashcroft flew down to give a 25-minute speech reiterating his commitment to fighting pornography, especially online porn accessible to children.

Ashcroft has authorized new funds and loosened restrictions to push into action the Child Exploitation and Obscenity Section, the Justice Department arm for prosecuting obscenity. "We may not be able to eradicate completely the criminal behavior associated with obscenity, but we can and we will change the pattern of behavior with aggressive law enforcement," he said in his address.

And as the Justice Department gets increasingly active in prosecuting obscenity, it may finally push the judiciary into answering the tough questions: What's the future of *Miller* in a cyberworld without communities? Can an Internet porn law ever pass constitutional muster? As more kids log on, what choices do parents have?

The anti-porn activists have yet to find an answer, but thanks to continued support in Congress, they may have one eventually. "We're not going to go away, and Congress is not going to stop passing these bills, Taylor says. "They may beat us now, but one of these bills will stick. The ACLU is doing a good job holding our feet to the fire, but the pendulum will eventually swing the other way."

LIBRARIES SHOULD USE SOFTWARE FILTERS TO CENSOR INTERNET PORNOGRAPHY

Robert Peters

Robert Peters is the president of the watchdog organization Morality in Media, which works to implement public policy against obscenity and excessive violence on the Internet and in other media. The following selection is taken from a speech Peters gave at a public forum at Staten Island, New York, on September 23, 1999. As Peters explains, he believes that installing software filters on public-access computers is the best way to protect children from Internet pornography. While he admits that the filtering programs may not be perfect, Peters maintains that they offer the most efficient method of blocking access to cyberporn in public and school libraries.

Clearly, there are many types of Internet content that can harm minors, including materials providing instructions on how to commit suicide, commit murder and make bombs and promoting violence against individuals because of their race, ethnic origin, religion, etc. Due to shortness of time, however, I am confining my remarks this evening to the problem of minors accessing Internet porn.

Exercising Discretion

Good librarians have a difficult job. On the one hand, they must be responsive to the needs and desires of the communities they serve. On the other hand, they cannot be expected to please everyone in the community all of the time. A good librarian knows when to please and when to fight.

But one thing is certain, librarians have historically exercised discretion in their selection of materials for inclusion in local libraries. They have done so both because of economic restraints and because of content considerations. To my knowledge, no public library has a large, prominent selection of anti-semitic or racist materials in order to encourage the public to read.

Nor, to my knowledge, has any library acquired a generous selection of videos, magazines and paperback books from local "adult bookstores." Such materials have no serious artistic, literary, political or scientific value, would be deeply offensive to the large majority of citizens, and can be harmful to both adults and children. They would also be a waste of tax dollars.

Now, along comes the Internet. Anyone who knows anything about the Internet knows that it has great potential to benefit and enrich human life. Anyone who knows anything about the Internet also knows that it has great potential to cause incalculable harm to nations, businesses and individuals, adults and children.

Why then, do most public libraries refuse to use screening technology to block minors' access to pornography?

First and foremost is the Library Bill of Rights of the ALA [American Library Association], which was adopted in 1948. I received a copy of it from the Brooklyn Library in the 1980s. That copy states, in part:

A PERSON'S RIGHT TO USE A LIBRARY SHOULD NOT BE DENIED OR ABRIDGED BECAUSE OF AGE. . . .

What this has been interpreted to mean is that if a parent peruses or checks out a book or video containing numerous prurient passages or scenes which depict or describe in a patently offensive manner hardcore sex acts, so can the children.

When I was a child, this provision made little difference, even if a local librarian was foolish enough to blindly apply it. Back then, most mainstream publishers had standards, videos hadn't been invented and bona fide sex education materials differed significantly from porn. And back then, to access the "worst stuff" in the library would often have required an ability to read and do research. At least younger children were protected.

Today, of course, things are different. The quantity of sexually explicit, often pornographic material within the four walls of public libraries has increased immeasurably and much more of it is pictorial. In some cases, it is even prominently displayed so that an ability to do research is not needed.

Minors and Internet Pornography

Most libraries also now provide unrestricted access to the Internet, which offers—free of charge—hardcore pornographic materials, some of which are so depraved you won't even find them sold in "adult" book and video stores.

And minors do access porn on the Internet. A Yankelovich Partners poll published in the May 10, 1999 issue of *Time* found that 44% of teen Internet users had seen web sites that "are X-rated or carry sexual content." Another Yankelovich Partners poll released [on September 7, 1999] found that 25 percent of teen Internet users said they went to

"X-rated" sex sites. Among teens with lower grades (C–F) or poor school attendance, the percentage rose to 34 percent. Of teens who accessed "objectionable" sites (porn, gambling, hate-group, offensive music, etc.), 79 percent accessed the sites from school computers.

But even children who aren't seeking porn can be exposed to it. Using a search engine to type in innocent words like toys, kitty, games or teen can lead children to the worst of web porn sites.

Some Internet pornographers purposefully use words like whitehouse, Titanic or Madonna in their web addresses or metatags to attract innocent seekers.

Other Internet pornographers use domain names that are extremely similar to those of high traffic web sites, like Beanie Babies, knowing many users will mistype the popular names.

Some web sites that carry ads for sites that are "X-rated" purposefully attract children by linking their own sites to sites intended for children. They do so because they get a fee each time someone clicks one of their ads for an "adult" sex site. That young children are unable to purchase the porn is irrelevant because once a child clicks the ad, the site gets a fee.

There are also pedophiles who use the Internet to contact children through chat rooms. A favorite tool of pedophiles is porn, which is used to desensitize and instruct their child victims.

I should add that the ALA's "Library Bill of Rights" is not the same thing as the Constitution's Bill of Rights. New York City libraries are not required by any law to follow the ALA version.

Problems with Anti-Filter Arguments

Another excuse given for not using screening technology is that it erroneously blocks some sites that are not pornographic. This happens, but screening technology continues to improve, and there are many different technologies to choose from. Libraries can and should also implement a review policy so that sites improperly blocked can be promptly unblocked.

Another excuse that libraries give for not using screening technology is that it provides a false sense of security because no technology can block all Internet sites containing pornographic materials. No screening technology is perfect, but some screening technologies are much more effective than others in blocking porn. Furthermore, there is no one method that can provide perfect protection, but combined with other safeguards (such as positioning computers so that screens are easily seen by a librarian or teacher, monitoring usage and enforcing rules), screening technology can help greatly to reduce minors' access to porn.

I would add that the ALA apparently talks through both sides of its mouth. In arguing that the 1996 Communications Decency Act (CDA), which would have required Internet content providers to restrict minors' access to indecent material, was unconstitutional, the ALA in its joint brief to the U.S. Supreme Court stated:

> The CDA is also unconstitutional because there are less restrictive measures Congress could have selected that would have been much *more* effective in preventing minors from gaining access to indecent online material. The district court made extensive findings about the ability of user-based [screening] software . . . to prevent children from accessing indecent material, regardless of where it is posted [on the Internet].

Another argument that has been made for not using screening technology is that it is not the job of public libraries to act "in loco parentis." In other words, when parents send or allow their children to go to tax dollar supported public libraries, they should not expect librarians to care any more about their children than the pornographers. In fact, they should expect less, because pornographers must obey obscenity and child porn laws, but the ALA typically lobbies to exempt public libraries from these laws.

Once again librarians talk through both sides of their mouths. They say that the First Amendment applies to libraries because libraries are agencies of state and local governments. But if libraries are government agencies, by what authority do librarians tell the public that it is not their job to act "in loco parentis?"

Yet another excuse for not using screening technology is that the First Amendment prevents libraries from doing so. As I see it, the First Amendment does not require public libraries to provide unlimited Internet access to patrons. The purpose of public libraries is to further public education and research and to provide a means of preserving valuable materials that would otherwise be lost to future generations. Libraries can under the Constitution adopt Internet policies consistent with that historic purpose. By adopting such policies, libraries would not have to concern themselves much about obscenity or child porn laws because access would only be provided to Internet sites containing material with serious artistic, literary, political or scientific value.

Protecting Minors from Harm

The last excuse I will address this evening is that there is no need for technology since there is no conclusive proof that minors are harmed by exposure to porn. Most minors probably aren't seriously harmed by exposure to porn because they have the good sense and inner strength to turn from it.

But the evidence is overwhelming that exposure to pornography can and does cause harm to many youth and to many adults; and in two leading cases, one involving materials obscene for adults [*Paris Adult Theater I v. Slaton*, 1973] and the other materials obscene for minors [*Ginsberg v. New York*, 1967], the Supreme Court rejected the argument that conclusive scientific proof is required before government can regulate obscenity.

I conclude by saying that I do not view screening technology as the whole answer to children accessing Internet porn. I do see it is an essential element, especially in a day when parents, churches and schools all too often fail to impart sound values and character to youth; when ISPs [Internet Service Providers] refuse to do all they can to block or restrict access to injurious content on the Internet; and when government fails to enforce federal and state obscenity laws.

More than any other single factor, President [Bill] Clinton's failure to fulfill his 1992 campaign pledge to make "vigorous" enforcement of federal obscenity laws "a priority" has allowed the Internet to become a safe haven for hardcore pornographers.

No nation which allows its culture to become an open sewer can hope to totally protect its children from the deadly waste, whether floating on the surface or hidden in underlying currents.

Libraries Should Not Use Software Filters to Censor the Internet

Electronic Frontier Foundation

The Electronic Frontier Foundation is an organization that works to protect privacy and freedom of expression on the Internet. The following selection is excerpted from a statement the foundation made to Congress in opposition to legislation requiring public and school libraries to install Internet filtering software on their computers. The purpose of such software is to protect children from sexually explicit material. However, according to the foundation, the software is ineffective and results in various violations of Americans' free-speech rights, including their right to read constitutionally protected material. In May 2002, a federal court in Philadelphia ruled the legislation unconstitutional.

Around the end of October 2000, Senator John McCain, Representative Ernest Istook, various other legislators, and the White House, cut a deal to include a controversial and misguided mandatory library content filtering "rider" on a major Labor, HHS & Education appropriations bill, H.R. 4577 (which was in House/Senate conference committee for months, and passed by Congress earlier in December.)

Legislators McCain and Istook, among several others, have for three years pushed various versions of legislation to grant Federal Communications Commission (FCC) regulatory control over the Internet and to force public and private libraries (and schools) that receive any of several federal funding sources to install Internet content filtering software, or else be denied a variety of vital federal funding (including Elementary and Secondary Education Act Title III ["Focused On Technology"], Library Services and Technology Act, and E-Rate funds [discounts on technology such as Internet access]). Istook's version in the House and McCain's version in the Senate were attached to H.R. 4577 before the bill passed to the conference committee. Both were removed with all other "riders" (small bills attached to a large one in hopes that they'll pass as part of the major bill).

Electronic Frontier Foundation, statement on H.R. 4577, Mandatory Censorware Provisions, December 22, 2000.

While the concerns raised, across the political spectrum, about this legislation probably had little impact on the rider removal decision, many expected the censorware proposal to die at this point (until 2001, at least). But, the chairman of the conference committee offered the disputing McCain and Istook the opportunity to hammer out a joint version of the filtering language. This was done, and the new result was put back in the bill. After further refinements to satisfy the President and VP, passage into law is virtually guaranteed, since the larger funding measure has passed with this rider.

At this juncture, the "Child Internet Protection Act" and "Neighborhood Child Internet Protection Act" (two related provisions of the filtering legislation) will have to be challenged in court, on First Amendment and other grounds.

The legislation is broadly opposed by liberal, conservative and non-partisan organizations, from the American Civil Liberties Union (ACLU) and the American Library Association to the Eagle Forum and the Christian Coalition. Congress's own Child Online Protection Act Commission rejected mandatory filtering in their recommendations to the legislature in November 2000.

Despite some early religious-right support for the notion of censorware, conservative groups now raise virtually identical concerns with this legislation as their liberal counterparts. A right-wing coalition letter to key legislators stated, "[t]here is growing concern within the conservative community regarding the use of filtering systems by schools and libraries that deliberately filter out web sites and information that promote conservative values. There have been many reported incidents of schoolteachers and administrators targeting . . . pro-life organizations with filtering software to prevent students from hearing alternative approaches to those issues." One begins to wonder just who, outside of a handful of legislators (and censorware marketers), believes in censorware any more.

A Problematic Proposal

For several years Congress has sought to impose some form of mandatory or "pseudo-voluntary" content filtering on all public libraries and public schools. The idea seems to sound nice to legislators and to a large segment of the general public, because they simply do not understand how the technology works (and, more importantly, how it fails to work.) The principal problems with the proposal are inherent in the software and services themselves. These include:

(a) subjective filtering criteria, in which a software company (i.e. a government contractor, subject to the First Amendment) gets to decide broadly what is and is not available to some or all library patrons via library Internet terminals;

(b) biased (typically politically-motivated) filtering decisions, in which software company employees or their consultants (who are again covered by First Amendment requirements because they are doing a job for the government), choose to block material that is not even covered by any stated filtering criteria of the product/service in question; such biases have blocked everything from EFF's own site to gay-rights news stories to Christian church Web pages;

(c) harm to the First Amendment–protected right to read, in an unprecedented system in which unaccountable software companies deny access to materials that are constitutionally protected (including material that no court has ever deemed indecent, obscene, or harmful to minors, as well as content not restricted by any legal category at all, such as "intolerant" material;

(d) mistaken blocking of innumerable sites as "pornographic", "violent", "intolerant" or otherwise "wrong", when in fact they contain no such content at all;

(e) mistaken blocking of names, non-vulgar words, and other material due to bad keyword matching algorithms;

(f) overly broad blocking in which entire directory structures or entire Web sites with thousands of users/authors are wholly blocked for content only found on one page;

(g) alteration of content in mid-stream, often in such a way as to either leave no indication that material has been censored, or to make the material nonsensical because material has been removed (e.g., in mid-sentence); this technique also raises issues of author's copyright-derived rights to control the distribution of "derivative works", when their words are "sanitized" by filtering software;

(h) provision of few (in many cases, no) options for selecting blocking criteria other than those pre-configured in the software; imposition of censorware would effectively force everyone to adhere to someone else's morality, in clear violation of the Freedom of Religion clause;

(i) dismal ineffectiveness at actually doing what they are advertised to do (block out sexually explicit and certain other kinds of content); no filtering service or product on the market has anywhere near even a 90% effectiveness rate, resulting in a completely false sense of security, and a "solution" that fixes nothing at all;

(j) blocking of materials that are constitutionally protected even for minors, as well as for adults;

(k) imposition of technological censorship measures that have already been ruled unconstitutional, in the *Mainstream Loudoun v. Loudoun Co.* [Virginia] *Library* case.

Costly, Dangerous, and Ineffective

Seth Finkelstein, the programmer principally responsible for the investigation of X-Stop filtering software and its flaws, vital to the landmark *Mainstream Loudoun* victory, observes: "The claims made by censorware vendors are technologically absurd and mathematically impossible. If people argue endlessly over what is art, how can a shoddy computer program ever have an answer? Imagine if a bigoted organization could, at the touch of a button, secretly remove from a school or library all books they deemed objectionable. That is the reality of censorware. This is book-burning on the Internet, by unaccountable blacklisters." In short, censorware simply does not perform as advertised, and substitutes simple-minded algorithms and a faceless one-size-fits-all morality for complex, context-dependent and highly personal human judgement. It does not get the job done, and the cost to library patrons' freedom to read (and authors' rights, as well) is far too great to bear for such a broken so-called solution to a problem (minors' access to inappropriate material) that is, at heart, one of parental rule-setting and oversight, not federal government regulation.

There are additional political problems that arise with such a proposal including:

1) It is an unfunded mandate that will ironically cost libraries more to implement than they will receive in federal funding in many cases (especially once all costs are included, such as software/service price, training, staff time dealing with complaints, consultant & system administration costs, and, of course, litigation).

2) It would usurp the responsibilities, and disregards the capabilities, of local libraries/library boards and state bodies to deal with these issues as local citizens demand. It would turn the Supreme Court–approved "community standards" content regulation system on its head, permitting the Federal government generally, and national and international corporations in great detail, to dictate what is and is not okay to read in city and county libraries.

3) It would impose a "one-size-fits-all" system of morality over the entire nation—precisely what the First Amendment exists to prevent—disallowing parental discretion and upsetting years of local efforts to set acceptable use policies and practices for libraries (over 90% of public libraries already have such policies in place).

4) It would turn librarians into snooping content police, and thereby threatens both the integrity of the library profession, and patron privacy.

5) It would hit hardest precisely those libraries that most need the withheld funding. Inner-city, rural and other low-income libraries would incur the most difficulty and expense to comply with the law, for the least returns, making it a lose-lose proposition.

6) It would use the definition of "harmful to minors" found in the Child Online Protection Act (COPA), which is currently under a federal injunction against enforcement on the grounds that it is most likely unconstitutional (pending the court's final decision).

7) It would "hard-code" into the law requirements for specific technologies that are both ineffective and likely to become obsolete within a very short timeframe (many believe they are already)—tech-

nologies incapable of anything remotely resembling human judgement. At the same time, it would disallow measures such as locally-
determined acceptable use policies, family education, or future technologies, as alternatives.

8) Last, but by no means least, it poses a severe threat to children's
privacy. The law would mandate the (ab)use of monitoring software
(which will necessarily entail detailed logs) to track minors' Internet
participation. While this is in and of itself draconian, the matter is far
worse than it seems at first. Courts are already deciding (as in the
James M. Knight v. Kingston NH School Administrative Unit No. 16 case)
that students' Internet logs are matters of public record. It is both
ironic and alarming that a law with "Children's Protection" in its title
would do more to harm minors than protect them.

The issues, thus, go far beyond the more obvious freedom of expression concerns. In a coalition letter to Congress from 17 educational
organizations (including National Education Association, National
PTA, and national principals' and school boards' associations) noted,
"[w]hile nearly every school in the United States already supervises
minors' online activity, promoting the use of technological monitoring software raises serious privacy and security concerns that have not
been examined by Congress. . . . Federal filtering mandates disregard
local policymaking prerogatives. Instead they require local decision-
makers to select among a few marketable national norms developed as
business plans by filtering software companies."

Devils in the Details

Aside from the general concerns raised above about the legislation as
a whole, there are many devils in the details. Some of the most troubling provisions of the bill are outlined below. Problems are listed as
they first appear. Many recur later in the legislation, much of which is
duplicative of previous sections, principally to make legal challenge
more difficult. (i.e., if we challenge the library provisions and have
them struck down, the school provisions still stand until separately
and successfully challenged on their own, unless a broad enough case
can be brought against all of the provisions at once.)

In Title I:

• The "DISABLING DURING ADULT USE" section imposes conditions that in effect require librarians to ascertain that an adult
patron's use of library computers is for "bona fide research or other
lawful purposes" before they are permitted to disable the filtering
software. If something like this should be done at all (which is highly
questionable), this is the job of a judge, not a librarian, and is a massive attack on patrons' privacy and right to read. Worse yet, filtering is
not required to be disabled by adult request (even after these impossible criteria are met); disabling is only "permitted", non-bindingly. As
if this were not bad enough, the language has a loophole that could

easily exclude actual librarians from having authority to turn off filters at all, requiring the approval of library administrators.

• The "GENERAL RULE" provision is worded such that NO ONE—not librarians, not even parents directly supervising their own children—may turn off the filters for a minor, no matter what it might be mis-blocking.

• The "GENERAL RULE" section also mandates that the software be able to block obscenity, child pornography and material harmful to minors. This is physically impossible—no software can determine what does or does not fall into these legal categories (only a court can), and cannot block even most let alone all of such material without blocking orders of magnitude more material than necessary (i.e. anything that *might* conceivably fall into such a category, and lots more besides). Censorware drags a very large net behind it.

• The "DEFINITIONS" section treats all persons under 17 years of age as if they were the same as 4-year-old children, making no distinction between maturity levels. The Supreme Court has already expressed grave concern with this legal concept, in reviewing "harmful to minors" laws. This new legislation raises this problem much more clearly than any previous laws.

• The "EFFECTIVE DATE" section gives libraries and schools only 120 days to comply with the impossible, or begin to lose funding unless they qualify for special extensions.

• The "OTHER MATERIALS" section permits (though does not require) libraries to block even more material (i.e., material that is not legally deemed obscene, harmful-to-minors or child-pornographic.) This is a recipe for outrageous amounts of needless litigation, and political attempts by censorious groups to seize control of library boards.

In Title II:

• Provision (iii) of the "INTERNET FILTERING" section appears to apply its requirements to private as well as public schools.

• The "CERTIFICATION WITH RESPECT TO ADULTS" section makes it clear that libraries are required to filter ALL library terminals even for adults (again, with a literally impossible requirement that the filters block certain legal categories that no software can accurately detect or identify). This section and the related one with regard to minors, require under no uncertain terms that libraries have and "enforce" policies to ensure that filters are on, used, and not bypassed. This turns librarians into spying Internet cops, violating both their own professional ethics and patrons' privacy. Resistant libraries will immediately be punished by the "FAILURE TO COMPLY WITH CERTIFICATION" clause: "Any [school or library] that knowingly fails to ensure the use of its computers in accordance with [the censorware mandate] shall reimburse all funds received in violation thereof."

In Title III:

• This additional section, the rather inexplicably named "Neighborhood Children's Internet Protection Act", requires stringent acceptable use policies (aspects of which are federally pre-ordained) for local school and library computer usage, in addition to, rather than as an alternative to, mandatory censorware.

• The deceptive "LOCAL DETERMINATION OF CONTENT" section has three major problems, the first of which is that the federal government is in fact establishing standards of what must be blocked even though the section title says it isn't. Secondly, this provision is a blanket encouragement of more conservative library and school districts' violation of the First Amendment with impunity by blocking anything they want. Third, even the vague and lax restraints that there would be on federal dictating of content regulations are put on hold until mid-2001.

• The "STUDY" section is ironic and hypocritical in requiring an NTIA study "evaluating whether or not currently available commercial internet [sic] blocking and filtering software adequately addresses the needs of educational institutions . . . and . . . evaluating the development and effectiveness of local Internet use policies that are currently in operation after community input." This should have been done BEFORE, not after, considering mandatory censorware laws! The study would also make "recommendations on how to foster the development of" more censorware—highly questionable as something to be legitimately done at taxpayer expense.

• The "IMPLEMENTING REGULATIONS" section gives the Federal Communications Commission the authority and responsibility of implementing the new law. This is probably the real, hidden purpose of the legislation—to give the FCC authority to regulate the Internet like it regulates (censors and permits oligopolistic control of) broadcasting. There is big and particularly anti-democratic corporate money lurking behind this measure. The one and only good thing anywhere in this legislation is a requirement for expedited court review, similar to the review provision in the Communications Decency Act, which enabled the EFF/(ACLU)/(CIEC) [Citizens Internet Empowerment Coalition] legal effort to overturn the CDA on constitutional grounds rapidly, before much harm was done.

A Rating System Can Protect Children from Websites with Adult Content

SafeSurf

Founded in 1995, SafeSurf is an organization dedicated to preventing childhood exposure to Internet pornography without resorting to censorship. In the following selection, SafeSurf contends that while children can be harmed by exposure to pornography on the Internet, official censorship will not protect children and could grant too much power to the government. Furthermore, software filtering programs are often ineffective at censoring online material, the organization maintains. As an alternative, SafeSurf advocates a rating system that would allow schools, libraries, and parents to identify any websites that are inappropriate for children. The organization proposes that Internet publishers assign websites various ratings to identify the level of adult content, much like Hollywood labels movies for viewers.

The Internet has grown by leaps and bounds in recent years because mass consensus has been reached on implementing many standards such as the World Wide Web and the HTML programming language. However, in order to keep the Internet from being consumed by the very information it provides, a consensus *must* be reached on how this information will be shared.

Unless we actively make decisions *now* as a responsible group, the right to make these decisions will be forever taken from us by our government.

The Importance of Classification

SafeSurf is dedicated to both advancing the process of classifying information on the Internet and enabling us, as a community, to gain the benefits that it will bring.

Our first goal is to classify material which may be harmful to children. This classification would allow anyone on the Internet to choose the type of information they will be receiving prior to it reaching their computer. Responsible choices can then be easily made and systems can be put into place that will screen adult material, restricting the access to minors.

The purpose of this classification system is not to censor. Rather, it is to provide an informed choice to each individual on the Internet.

There is more to be gained than just the free flow of information. This information classification system will enable software and hardware to be developed that will enable more effective use of the Internet for everyone.

SafeSurf proposes a classification system involving a code consisting of a type description and number. The typing would specify the nature of the information (sexual, violent), whereas the number would represent the level of intensity of the description. The number directly corresponds with the level of parental awareness. The higher the number, the more caution parents should exercise in permitting children to access this information.

The Online Cooperative Publishing Act

Any law that seeks to regulate the Internet must first recognize the uniqueness of the medium. The Internet is not the print media or the broadcast industry. It is also not another form of phone conversation or a 900 number calling system. Instead, the Internet is the manifestation of humankind's quest for limitless two-way interaction with thought. The hyper-text layout allows us to change topics on a whim, travel to distant places, or gather world opinion on a subject in a matter of minutes.

This distinctive nature of the Internet must be protected and even promoted by any legislation that claims to be fair to this medium. The interaction between the one receiving data and the one publishing it is where the core of the law should focus. Both sides have rights: the publisher has the First Amendment and the receiver has the right to be secure from harm in his home. Proper Internet law should encourage a cooperative transfer of ideas in the form of data. (It should be noted that it was the universal acceptance of basic roles of cooperation, rather than anarchy, that built the Internet.)

Any law that attempts to give one side or the other an unreasonable burden in conducting the transfer of data is doomed to failure. The Communications Decency Act (CDA) was too burdensome on the publisher. Its goal was to stop the flow of data, rather than to regulate the transfer for the benefit of all parties.

On the other hand, without a proper law, parents can purchase and activate measures to protect their children from adult material and still not feel secure in their homes from unwanted material. This is because negligent publishing of data eventually allows material that can harm the child to enter the home. Once this material is experienced by the child, the damage is done. There is no "oops" factor, no way to undo the unwanted intrusion into a child's innocence.

Most importantly, any Internet law must not censor thought. It may regulate the labeling on the packaging but never the content.

With the goal of achieving a greater spirit of cooperation between the publisher and the receiver of online data, we propose the Online Cooperative Publishing Act.

The Provisions of the Act

It shall contain the following provisions:

1. The right to be able to identify the adult rating of online content before it enters one's home shall be established. This shall be a civil right giving the violated person or family the presumption in a suit against negligent publishers.

2. Negligent publishing of data shall be defined as placing adult oriented material on the Internet in such a way or in such a location that it prevents its rating from being known.

3. A rating shall be defined as a PICS compatible label that identifies degrees of adult content in a way that can be understood by computer filtering systems and is issued by a ratings service that has a minimum of 5,000 documented individuals using its system to mark their data. [PICS, or Platform for Internet Content Selection, allows a blank label to be inserted into web page content. Then a rating can be attached to that label.]

4. A publisher is defined as anyone who places computer data where it can be accessed by the general public without the use of a credit card or other secure verified ID or password given out only to adults. Content that can only be accessed by the use of credit cards or other secure verified IDs is not subject to this law. (Note: Web pages containing "free samples" of pornographic material presented by secure adult sites must be rated.)

5. The code used to surround content published on the Internet shall be defined as packaging. All government identification requirements shall be limited to the code of the packaging. Nothing in this law shall be construed to require any altering or censorship of the content.

6. Three types of online publishing shall be defined:

a) *Publishers who accurately identify data with a recognized labeling system.* These publishers shall be considered to have satisfied the labeling requirement of the law. The right to publish shall be completely protected for those who accurately label their material. They shall be protected from all civil suits that argue negligent posting of data. Only grossly mislabeled material can be prosecuted. (Note: This is not a protection for obscene material. This law will offer no protection for obscene material. Anything illegal off the Internet shall be illegal on the Internet.)

b) *Publishers who mislabel their data to the degree that it enables a minor using a label filtering system to gain access to harmful material.* Publishers who recklessly mislabel may be criminally prosecuted for subverting a rating system to entice children to harmful material. The mislabeling must be to the extent that it is completely unreasonable to accept it as accurate. Only ratings that are too lenient can be prosecuted.

Data shall be considered to be mislabeled if it is posted in a newsgroup, directory or other joint area that has been labeled as free from material harmful to minors. Posting unlabeled adult material to an area that has declared itself safe for children shall be considered a criminal assault on the rights of the receiver.

Tampering with another's label shall be criminal offense. This type of vandalism violates the rights of both the publisher and the receiver.

Sending unsolicited email that contains pornographic material or an invitation to a pornographic Web Site to a minor, shall be considered negligent enticement and may be fined. A bulk email service sending pornographic email must show that it took reasonable measures to insure that every, recipient was an adult. (Example: The addresses used were from the membership list of Adult Check or other such adult verification services.)

c) *Publishers who do not label their data at all.* Negligence in the absence of damages may be a civil violation of the rights of the receivers of that data, but it shall not be a criminal offense unless the data is deemed to be harmful to minors. Then the publisher may be prosecuted for negligence.

Publishers may be sued in civil court by any parent who feels their children were harmed by the data negligently published. The parents/plantiffs shall be given presumption, if the case involves graphic images, and do not have to prove that the content actually produced harm to their child, only that the material was severe enough to reasonably be considered to have needed a rating label to protect children.

When content consists of words alone, the presumption would rest with the publisher. Additionally, in a suit consisting only of "offending language", the publisher would be entitled to seek damages, if the plaintiffs fail to prove their case.

However, before any legal action can be taken, the offending publisher must be notified by the plaintiff that it is publishing content that needs to be rated and where to obtain a label. The publisher must be given a reasonable time to comply.

The plantiffs have the burden to prove that the purpose of the content was not medical, encyclopedic, nor news.

Liabilities and Penalties

7. Internet Service Providers are considered publishers of only that material of which they directly control or gain revenue via a percentage of sales. Web Site designers may be held liable if they fail to attach ratings to Web sites they produce that contain material harmful to

minors. They may, by written agreement, assign the task of rating to another legally responsible party.

8. Not every document is required to be labeled, only the default or index document of each directory. In the case of an entire web domain being of one rating, only its default top level document needs to be labeled with instructions to apply it to the entire site.

9. The penalty for a first offense of failing to label or mislabeling material harmful to minors shall be limited to a fine of under five thousand dollars. Larger fines and incarceration shall be applicable to only those who are chronic violators. Altering another's label to enable harmful material to be viewed by minors shall be felony on the first offense.

CYBERLITERACY: AN ALTERNATIVE TO CENSORSHIP

Laura J. Gurak

When trying to find a solution to the problem of encountering offensive or potentially harmful material while surfing on the Internet, many people recommend censoring or filtering offensive websites. Laura J. Gurak proposes an alternative to blocking offensive material: cyberliteracy. She suggests that Internet users become cyberliterate—that is, they should learn how to distinguish between legitimate informational sites and those that contain misinformation and extremist hate speech. Internet users who recognize the difference can combat offensive and deceptive websites by speaking out against them rather than censoring them, Gurak maintains, thus preserving the right to free expression while promoting critical thinking and discussion. Gurak is a professor of rhetoric at the University of Minnesota in Minneapolis–St. Paul. She has written several books about cyberspace, including *Cyberliteracy: Navigating the Internet with Awareness*, from which the following excerpt is taken.

For the past several years, as computers have become cheaper and anyone can suddenly become a desktop publisher, we have witnessed a rise of extremist Web sites in the United States. In these cases, we see an extreme version of flaming [the hostile expression of strong emotions] and, in addition, the dark side of online community. Community, one aspect of reach, can be a powerful way for people with similar interests to come together and share ideas. Many observers have noticed the power of online community not only to reach out to the world but also to create cohesion and solidarity among a regional community. Yet the ability to link with like-minded people and form community can have a dangerous side. Because of the power of speed and reach, and because of the value we place on free speech (a right of U.S. citizens and one that pervades the ethos of cyberspace), extremist Web sites exist side by side with all the millions of other Web displays, all equally available with just a few keystrokes.

To some extent, these sites reflect an anger and disempowerment that have become noticeable in the United States at this time. Domestic terrorism is at an all-time high, and angry people, primarily white males, are banding together like never before. These groups can hide behind a Web site, with its wide reach, relying on the power of anonymity to keep them from the people they don't wish to face. Yet in terms of cyberliteracy, these sites are frightening because their messages are hateful, angry, and violent in tone.

How can we judge these sites in an attempt to think about cyberliteracy? The first and most obvious way is to consider them in legalistic terms.

Unprotected Speech

The prevailing legal standard is based on the liberal enlightenment model (the foundation for philosophy and laws of free speech in the United States) and holds that all ideas should be given equal voice in the press and other information media. In this model, it is expected that citizens will in the end weed out good ideas from the bad. This model has generally functioned well, in part because it is hard to think of alternatives: censorship rarely works for any length of time, and in an electronic age censorship is even more difficult to enforce. Ever since the Tiananmen Square uprising in China during the spring of 1989, when information flowed outward via fax and the Internet (despite government attempts to control it), it has become evident that information is global, not local—or, as some hackers like to say, "information wants to be free."

But despite this emphasis on free speech in the United States and on the Internet, some speech is simply not legally protected. The standard by which the courts make this decision is based on the idea that certain words can be dangerous and harmful to people. It uses the standard of "shouting fire in a crowded theater": Would the speech bring about violence against others? Language that incites violence is often ruled as unprotected. It is upon this standard that we currently make legal decisions about hate speech and the Internet.

One example that illustrates how the legal standard can be used to judge an extremist site is the case of the Nuremberg Files, a Web site created by an anti-abortion group. This site used "Wanted"-style posters to list the names, addresses, and license plate numbers of physicians who performed abortions. The Web page was designed with a special interactive feature: when a physician on the list was killed, his or her name was struck through with a red line. On 2 February 1999 a federal district court ruled that this site was not protected speech. The jury determined that the site was intended to incite violence and murder; one piece of telling evidence was the listing of Dr. Barnett Slepian, a physician from Buffalo, New York, who was murdered and whose name had a line drawn through it on the Web site.

Web sites and other online discourse (email messages, Usenet post-ings) can thus be judged according to their legality. By legal standards the Nuremberg Files Web site was not acceptable. It was not protected speech because it incited physical violence and death; with the wide reach of Web pages, this standard is important to uphold. Online stalking can also be judged by legal standards. When one woman spurned a male co-worker's sexual advances, he posted notes on the Internet that looked as though they were being posted by her. These notes included the woman's address, phone number, and information about her home security system. They also suggested that she had fantasies about being raped. Through the power of reach, these notes spread over the Internet. Legally, this action was judged unacceptable: in January 1999 a judge in Los Angeles convicted the man under a new anti-stalking state law.

Anti-Information

Many other sites may represent legal, protected speech but would be considered disturbing to the average person. Anti-Semitic, racist, or homophobic sites that encourage paranoia, anger, and hate can fall into this category. Most of us can spot the obvious ones, such as sites asserting that the Holocaust never happened, or sites that encourage overt bigotry or racism. But some sites are less obvious, and this layer of sites must be carefully examined if we are to consider the meaning of cyberliteracy. Many of these sites masquerade as informational, adopting the format and style of a newspaper, report, or other truly informational setting. They use professional-looking fonts, high-quality layouts, and other credibility-boosting devices that are easy to employ on the Web. But to be cyberliterate means to be able to look past the format. Just because a site looks good or seems neutral and informational does not mean it is so. The powerful visual tools (fonts, layout, graphics) of the Web make everything look "real," and the ability to link to other sites enhances this sense of credibility. As one commentary noted, "racist pages are growing in sophistication and may lure the unwary."

Therefore, a different, cyberliterate way to view Web sites is not only via a legal standard but also via a moral one. Although most forms of speech are protected, not all forms of speech are morally or ethically acceptable. An event from my electronic life makes this argument.

Informational vs. Extremist Sites

One morning, innocently enough, a discussion began on our depart-ment email list that soon became a perfect case for analyzing the trend of calling clearly biased sites "informational." That morning, our College Career Services director posted a note announcing that representatives from AmeriCorps, the volunteer program for college students, would be visiting campus.

As mentioned earlier, what is especially disturbing about many extremist sites is that they pretend to be informational. Yet by now, most people who teach or theorize about writing know that there is no such thing as purely informational writing. Instead, we know that all language has a voice and an opinion, and that all language wields power. So when a student suggested that a site linked to the philosophies of Ayn Rand was a valid counterpoint to the posting about AmeriCorps, I was moved to get into the debate.

When I viewed the suggested site, I was immediately disturbed. It was apparent that this site was not simply a "source of information" to use for comparison with the posting about AmeriCorps. It was an extremist view, unbalanced and revealing an underlying ethos of anger and hate. I felt compelled to post a note indicating that such an extremist site was not a good counterpoint, and in my note, I also injected a bit of opinion about Ayn Rand's objectivist movement. After all, an academic list is a site of free speech, and as an Internet critic with a cyberliteracy agenda, I feel it's important to make strong claims to counter the prevailing winds of commercialism and individualism pervading the Internet. Like many departments, we often have such exchanges on our mailing list. My email set off a flurry of messages, mostly in response to my classifying the site as a "hate site." Some students saw the obvious connections, but others were not convinced, swayed as they were by the look and feel of the site: nice graphics, a supposedly bona fide organization, links to other sources, and so on. Yet a quick analysis shows that this site shares many features with the more overt extremist sites. In some ways, examining this site is more useful than looking at the more overt ones, because such an examination illustrates the subtlety needed for cyberliteracy.

An Analysis of the Site

This site, purportedly sponsored by advocates of objectivism, is more subtle than sites often classified as extremist, because at first glance it does not seem to employ overtly hateful tactics. But as with many extremist sites, this one uses an informational mode to disguise its message as credible; for example, it employs traditionally informative genres, such as press releases and position papers. Also, the page has a nice design and an appealing layout. Yet a quick analysis identifies this site as one inspired primarily by anger, not facts. The largest and most prominent image on the page is a photo of a group of protesters holding signs featuring such extreme language as "slavery" and "Nazi." Many extremist sites associate themselves with Nazism in some way, and even though this site is using the term to describe AmeriCorps, the word itself is evocative of hatefulness.

Moreover, the association of AmeriCorps with "forced servitude" illustrates a hyperbolic, paranoid, angry ethos, one that is often evident on extremist sites. The very premise that the AmeriCorps program equals "forced servitude" is flawed, because AmeriCorps is a volunteer program: no one is forced to join. Real servitude, as in slavery, is quite a different thing from joining AmeriCorps, the Peace Corps, or any other volunteer organization.

Like most extremist sites, this one exhibits the following characteristics:

- *Anger.* Most extremist sites are set up to vent anger. Unfortunately, the people who create these pages often fail to realize that anger inspires action. Words like *Nazi, slavery,* and *servitude* do not inspire open discussion; instead, they make those who believe those words even more angry, and they make those who don't hold this point of view upset as well.
- *Paranoia.* It is common on these sites to read about government conspiracies; for example, this site refers to President Bill Clinton's views as "call[s] for American servitude."
- *Mob or group action.* Most extremist sites inspire mob action. In this case, the crowd of students in the photo feels more like a mob than a peaceful protest because of the angry messages on their signs and the exaggerated use of "Nazi" and "slavery."
- *Hyperbolic claims.* Extremist sites usually make exaggerated claims. Suggesting that AmeriCorps is "forced servitude," for example, is baseless, because no one is forced to volunteer for the organization.
- *Self-referentiality* (citing and linking to similar groups). Extremist sites often provide links that look like outside information but actually connect to other like-minded thinkers. In this case, the links on the right side of the page are links to other materials from the Ayn Rand Institute.

In terms of cyberliteracy, a legal standard is of no use here, because this site does not directly suggest violence or harm to others. Shutting down this site because we do not agree with it is a bad idea and would certainly be a step on the slippery slope of censorship. Instead, the standard for cyberliteracy should be a critical one. To be cyberliterate in our system of free speech, we must learn to read, view, and think critically. We need to be aware that Web sites that are set up to sound "informational" always have a point of view, and that sometimes this point of view can be cause for concern, especially if it goes unexamined. Furthermore, although the Web constitutes a vast source of information, it is self-referential in a way that no other communication medium can be, because it can continually update its links. This self-referencing can be a problem: linking to similar ideas encourages a closed debate, one that does not admit conflicting viewpoints.

Filtering Out the Anger

The Anti-Defamation League (ADL), among other groups, has reported on what it calls "the dark side of the Internet"; in particular, the ADL is concerned about how hate sites can be used to recruit new followers, particularly young people. Many people who teach speech and writing have begun to notice that more and more students want to give a speech or write a paper about some "informational" topic, which turns out to be based on "information" from one of these hate sites ("proving," for example, that the Holocaust did not occur).

One approach to the problem is the use of filters, such as the ADL's HateFilter. Although filters can help, they have limits. Filters that search for the word *Nazi* can filter out accurate, scholarly information along with the extremist sites. Perhaps for young children, such filters are one tool parents can turn to. But for adults, a more useful filter begins with cyberliteracy, because cyberliteracy requires us to take more than just a legal stance when it comes to evaluating online spaces. It requires us to speak up when we encounter sites masquerading as informational and to teach our children, friends, students, and colleagues about the consequences of online anger. Furthermore, it requires us to counter these spaces by developing and supporting sites that embody inclusiveness, civility, and scholarly ideals.

Another approach is suggested by legal scholar and Internet theorist Lawrence Lessig. Lessig agrees that judging Web sites by legal standards alone is not enough. He makes this claim for a slightly different reason: because the Internet is global, laws about protected speech in one country are not the same as laws in another. Speech that promotes the Nazi party, for example, is illegal in Germany but not in the United States. Lessig argues that at the level of "code"—that is, by tinkering with browser software—individual users can customize their profile to filter out information they don't wish to see, and that this approach is preferable to broad governmental efforts to regulate speech. In the United States, one such effort was the Communications Decency Act of 1996, which Lessig calls "a law of extraordinary stupidity" and which was later overturned by the Supreme Court. This law would have regulated speech—particularly pornography—on the Internet. But the court rejected this approach, viewing it as too broad, vague, and dangerous to the first amendment.

Lessig is correct in arguing that laws should not and cannot be used to regulate speech online. Yet what his approach ignores is the very point made by my example of the AmeriCorps debate. Filters and personal profiles could, if refined from their current states (filters, in particular, still are not perfect), do a fine job of removing sites that you don't want to see before they ever reach your computer. But they enhance the ability of people to stay within their own communities, reading only the things that already support their frame of reference. The angry students who support the objectivist site could easily filter out any information that they find contrary and view only those sites that support their stance. The same thing would be true for everyone—people with liberal, communitarian, or left-wing viewpoints would read only what they like, people who are anti-abortion would encounter only those ideas that supported their frame of reference, and so on. And people who are already hostile would grow even angrier if all they encountered were hate and extremist sites. Filters, then, may have their place, but they do not support a full cyberliteracy, one that believes in open information but asks Internet citizens to turn a critical eye on whatever information they encounter.

Anger and Cyberliteracy

In the end, cyberliteracy means rejecting technological determinism. Even though the key features of online communication—speed, reach, anonymity, interactivity—may inspire or encourage us to behave in certain ways, in the end we, not the machines, are in charge. The edgy, wired times we live in do not necessarily have to translate into all-out anger. Cyberliteracy means understanding the tendencies of Internet communication and making thoughtful, informed choices. You can stop yourself from flaming someone just as you can stop yourself from saying something hateful in person. Many companies, organizations, and electronic lists or Web spaces have created rules of netiquette for their individual sites rather than succumbed to the draw of the technology.

Even if you do use filters, you should be aware of a range of discussions and points of view, and you should voice your opinion when you do not agree. Another approach might be to engage extremist sites in class exercises or as a topic of discussion at work or with your family. Because cyberspace has such a global reach, enhances communities over vast distances, and encourages discourse among lots of people, we need to learn more tolerance, not less. Cyberliteracy means being open but critical. Speak up. Create ways to assess online anger. Get away from the machine for a few minutes each day. Find ways to live in a world of ideas but not a world of hatred.

In addition, it is important to support legislation that helps increase the tolerance and goodwill of cyberspace. For example, the California law that makes online stalking a crime should be considered at a federal level, because currently only one-third of all states have such laws. And while laws can help, cyberliteracy also means being aware that computer technologies and the Internet are not neutral. We build our biases into technology, and we bring our social conditions into online space.

CHAPTER 4

GOVERNMENT CENSORSHIP

GOVERNMENT CENSORSHIP WOULD BE BENEFICIAL

Roger Kimball

In the following essay, Roger Kimball argues that government censorship of the graphic sex and violence produced by Hollywood would benefit society. Not only do images of brutal violence and explicit sex decrease the quality of art and entertainment, he states, but they also desensitize viewers. Constantly exposing children to these graphic images erodes their morals and imagination, Kimball maintains. Freedom of speech was never intended to protect such offensive and dangerous material, he concludes. Kimball is the managing editor of the *New Criterion* and an art critic for the London *Spectator*. His books include *Art's Prospect: The Challenge of Tradition in an Age of Celebrity* and *The Long March: How the Cultural Revolution of the 1960s Changed America*.

Isn't it time someone put in a good word for censorship? After pocketing his loot from the nice people in Hollywood, Sen. Joseph Lieberman assured them that "we will never, never put the government in the position of telling you by law, through law, what to make. We will noodge you, but we will never become censors." [Editor's note: Noodge is a Yiddish term for a gentle nag.]

Why not? As William Bennett pointed out, Sen. Lieberman sang a very different tune before he became Al Gore's running mate. He thundered against the "culture of carnage," and warned that if Hollywood continued "to market death and degradation to our children . . . then one way or another, the government will act."

What's wrong with a little censorship? Until quite recently, all sorts of things were censored in American society. There were very strict rules about what you could show on television and in movies, what you could describe in books and what you could reproduce in magazines. Were we worse off then?

Think about it. Not so long ago, you could turn on the television and be absolutely certain that you weren't going to be confronted with potty-mouthed people taking off their clothes. You could go down to the local newsstand and not see rows of pornography for sale. You could go to the movies and not worry about witnessing someone's viscera splashed across the screen. You could see commercials for Chesterfields on television, but the ads on buses were clearly distinguishable from pedophiliac fantasy. Was that a repressive time?

In some ways, yes. But is that sort of repression a bad thing? In my opinion, Sigmund Freud was wrong about almost everything. Yet he was right when he observed that civilization is founded on one very short word: *No*. Without what Freud called sublimation, you don't get civilization. Edmund Burke made a similar point: "Men are qualified for civil liberty," he said, "in exact proportion to their disposition to put moral chains on their own appetites. . . . Society cannot exist unless a controlling power upon will and appetite be placed somewhere, and the less of it there is within, the more there is without."

Just the other day, the *New York Times* ran a front-page story with the headline "Parents Say Censoring Films Is Their Job Not Politicians'." What rot! Parents can do absolutely nothing to censor the entertainment industry. And it is clear that the entertainment industry is not going to censor itself. As always, the people who run it will go exactly as far as the law allows them to go. In my opinion, the law currently allows them to go much too far.

Does that mean I am in favor of—gasp—government censorship? Sure. Would it be such a bad thing if pornography were a little harder to come by, if "gross-out" movies were a little less gross, if there were less violence on television? Believe me, the republic would survive.

And the right of free speech? Well, what about it? Recent court cases notwithstanding, the First Amendment was not framed in order to protect pornography or depictions of violence. Indeed, until the 1950s, the courts explicitly excluded free speech as a defense for trafficking in obscene materials. Are we better off now?

Even if one is an absolutist when it comes to the First Amendment, it is worth noting that the existence of a right to do something does not mean that it is a morally or socially acceptable thing to do. As John Searle, the philosopher, has observed, "any healthy human institution—family, state, university, ski team—grants its members rights that far exceed the bounds of morally acceptable behavior. . . . The gulf between the rights granted and the performance expected is bridged by the responsibility of the members." When that responsibility falters, society requires moral strictures and legal penalties to make up the difference.

It is also worth noting that many people who consider themselves First Amendment absolutists have no problem with the censorship that comes with political correctness. When you can lose your job and be subject to legal penalties because you tell a joke around the office water cooler, you are living in a very censorious society. Maybe we need a little less political correctness and a little more moral restraint.

In any event, there are plenty of reasons to support government censorship when it comes to depictions of sex and violence. For one thing, it would encourage the entertainment industry to turn out material that is richer erotically. This may seem paradoxical. But one problem with the almost-anything-goes attitude we have now is that it can make for boring and simplistic fare.

There is, if I remember correctly, only one kiss in Henry James's *The Golden Bowl*. But that novel communicates a deeper and more fully human eroticism than a book full of dirty words and the deeds they name.

It's the same in the movies. It is fashionable today to decry the old Hollywood code that proscribed showing even a married couple together in a double bed. But what a goad to imagination and cleverness that code turned out to be! Anyone who has seen Clark Gable and Claudette Colbert in *It Happened One Night*, or Myrna Loy and William Powell together in anything, knows that you do not need nudity or graphic language to make a sexy movie. On the contrary, if those movies had included what are euphemistically referred to as "adult situations," their charm, including their erotic charm, would have been killed.

Another reason to support government censorship is that it would help temper the extraordinary brutality of popular culture. Perhaps you have seen "studies" by some experts telling you that depictions of violence do not lead to violent behavior. Pay them no heed. Even if true, which I doubt, there can be no question that brutality brutalizes. It corrupts taste and poisons the imagination.

Society has an interest in protecting free speech and the free circulation of ideas. It also has an interest in protecting the moral sensibility of its citizens, especially the young. Freedom without morality degenerates into the servitude of libertinage. Which is why judicious government censorship is not the enemy of freedom but its guarantor.

GOVERNMENT CENSORSHIP WOULD BE HARMFUL

American Civil Liberties Union

The American Civil Liberties Union (ACLU) is a national organization that works to defend and preserve the individual rights guaranteed to all Americans by the U.S. Constitution. In the following selection, the ACLU argues that government censorship poses a much greater threat to society than any controversial images of sex or violence in art and entertainment. According to the organization, studies conducted on the potentially harmful effects of sex and violence in the media have produced no conclusive evidence. Furthermore, the authors warn, once the government is given the power to censor some types of entertainment, it will become increasingly difficult to determine where such censorship should stop. The appropriate way to handle offensive material in a democracy is to exercise the right to freedom of speech to explain why the material is objectionable, the ACLU contends.

In the late 1980s, state prosecutors brought a criminal obscenity charge against the owner of a record store for selling an album by the rap group, *2 Live Crew*. Although this was the first time that obscenity charges had ever been brought against song lyrics, the *2 Live Crew* case focused the nation's attention on an old question: should the government ever have the authority to dictate to its citizens what they may or may not listen to, read, or watch?

To Censor, or Not to Censor?

American society has always been deeply ambivalent about this question. On the one hand, our history is filled with examples of overt government censorship, from the 1873 Comstock Law to the 1996 Communications Decency Act. Anthony Comstock, head of the Society for the Suppression of Vice, boasted 194,000 "questionable pictures" and 134,000 pounds of books of "improper character" were destroyed under the Comstock Law—*in the first year alone.* The Communications Decency Act imposed an unconstitutional censorship scheme on the Internet, accurately described by a federal judge as "the most participatory form of mass speech yet developed."

On the other hand, the commitment to freedom of imagination and expression is deeply embedded in our national psyche, buttressed by the First Amendment, and supported by a long line of Supreme Court decisions.

Provocative and controversial art and in-your-face entertainment put our commitment to free speech to the test. Why should we oppose censorship when scenes of murder and mayhem dominate the TV screen, when works of art can be seen as a direct insult to people's religious beliefs, and when much sexually explicit material can be seen as degrading to women? Why not let the majority's morality and taste dictate what others can look at or listen to?

The answer is simple, and timeless: a free society is based on the principle that each and every individual has the right to decide what art or entertainment he or she wants—or does not want—to receive or create. Once you allow the government to censor someone else, you cede to it the power to censor you, or something you like. Censorship is like poison gas: a powerful weapon that can harm you when the wind shifts.

Freedom of expression for ourselves requires freedom of expression for others. It is at the very heart of our democracy.

Sexual Speech

Sex in art and entertainment is the most frequent target of censorship crusades. Many examples come to mind. A painting of the classical statue of Venus de Milo was removed from a store because the managers of the shopping mall found its semi-nudity "too shocking." Hundreds of works of literature, from Maya Angelou's *I Know Why the Caged Bird Sings* to John Steinbeck's *Grapes of Wrath*, have been banned from public schools based on their sexual content.

A museum director was charged with a crime for including sexually explicit photographs by Robert Mapplethorpe in an art exhibit.

American law is, on the whole, the most speech-protective in the world—but sexual expression is treated as a second-class citizen. No causal link between exposure to sexually explicit material and anti-social or violent behavior has ever been scientifically established, in spite of many efforts to do so. Rather, the Supreme Court has allowed censorship of sexual speech on moral grounds—a remnant of our nation's Puritan heritage.

This does not mean that all sexual expression can be censored, however. Only a narrow range of "obscene" material can be suppressed; a term like "pornography" has no legal meaning. Nevertheless, even the relatively narrow obscenity exception serves as a vehicle for abuse by government authorities as well as pressure groups who want to impose their personal moral views on other people.

Media Violence

Today's calls for censorship are not motivated solely by morality and taste, but also by the widespread belief that exposure to images of violence *causes* people to act in destructive ways. Pro-censorship forces, including many politicians, often cite a multitude of "scientific studies" that allegedly prove fictional violence leads to real-life violence.

There is, in fact, virtually no evidence that fictional violence causes otherwise stable people to become violent. And if we suppressed material based on the actions of unstable people, no work of fiction or art would be safe from censorship. Serial killer Theodore Bundy collected cheerleading magazines. And the work most often cited by psychopaths as justification for their acts of violence is the Bible.

But what about the rest of us? Does exposure to media violence actually lead to criminal or anti-social conduct by otherwise stable people, including children, who spend an average of 28 hours watching television each week? These are important questions. If there really were a clear cause-and-effect relationship between what normal children see on TV and harmful actions, then limits on such expression might arguably be warranted.

Studies on the relationship between media violence and real violence are the subject of considerable debate. Children have been shown TV programs with violent episodes in a laboratory setting and then tested for "aggressive" behavior. *Some* of these studies suggest that watching TV violence may temporarily induce "object aggression" in *some* children (such as popping balloons or hitting dolls or playing sports more aggressively) but not actual criminal violence against another person.

Correlational studies that seek to explain why some aggressive people have a history of watching a lot of violent TV suffer from the chicken-and-egg dilemma: does violent TV cause such people to behave aggressively, or do aggressive people simply prefer more violent entertainment? There is no definitive answer. But all scientists agree that statistical correlations between two phenomena do not mean that one causes the other.

International comparisons are no more helpful. Japanese TV and movies are famous for their extreme, graphic violence, but Japan has a very low crime rate—much lower than many societies in which television watching is relatively rare. What the studies reveal on the issue of fictional violence and real world aggression is—not much.

The only clear assertion that can be made is that the relationship between art and human behavior is a very complex one. Violent and sexually explicit art and entertainment have been a staple of human cultures from time immemorial. Many human behavioralists believe that these themes have a useful and constructive societal role, serving as a vicarious outlet for individual aggression.

What Does Artistic Freedom Include?

The Supreme Court has interpreted the First Amendment's protection of artistic expression very broadly. It extends not only to books, theatrical works and paintings, but also to posters, television, music videos and comic books—whatever the human creative impulse produces.

Two fundamental principles come into play whenever a court must decide a case involving freedom of expression. The first is "content neutrality"—the government cannot limit expression just because any listener, or even the majority of a community, is offended by its content. In the context of art and entertainment, this means tolerating some works that we might find offensive, insulting, outrageous— or just plain bad.

The second principle is that expression may be restricted only if it will clearly cause *direct and imminent* harm to an important societal interest. The classic example is falsely shouting fire in a crowded theater and causing a stampede. Even then, the speech may be silenced or punished only if there is no other way to avert the harm.

Whatever influence fictional violence has on behavior, most experts believe its effects are marginal compared to other factors. Even small children know the difference between fiction and reality, and their attitudes and behavior are shaped more by their life circumstances than by the books they read or the TV they watch. In 1972, the U.S. Surgeon General's Advisory Committee on Television and Social Behavior released a 200-page report, "Television and Growing Up: The Impact of Televised Violence," which concluded, "The effect [of television] is small compared with many other possible causes, such as parental attitudes or knowledge of and experience with the real violence of our society." Twenty-one years later, the American Psychological Association published its 1993 report, "Violence & Youth," and concluded, "The greatest predictor of future violent behavior is a previous history of violence." In 1995, the Center for Communication Policy at the University of California at Los Angeles (UCLA) which monitors TV violence, came to a similar conclusion in its yearly report: "It is known that television does not have a simple, direct stimulus-response effect on its audiences."

Blaming the media does not get us very far, and, to the extent that diverts the public's attention from the real causes of violence in society, it may do more harm than good.

A pro-censorship member of Congress once attacked the following shows for being too violent: *The Miracle Worker, Civil War Journal, Star Trek 9, The Untouchables,* and *Teenage Mutant Ninja Turtles.* What would be left if all these kinds of programs were purged from the airwaves? Is there good violence and bad violence? If so, who decides? Sports and the news are at least as violent as fiction, from the fights that erupt during every televised hockey game, to the videotaped beating of Rodney King by the LA Police Department, shown over and over again on prime time TV. If we accept censorship of violence in the media, we will have to censor sports and news programs.

Individual Rights, Individual Decisions

The First Amendment is based upon the belief that in a free and democratic society, individual adults must be free to decide for themselves what to read, write, paint, draw, see and hear. If we are disturbed by images of violence or sex, we can change the channel, turn off the TV, and decline to go to certain movies or museum exhibits.

We can also exercise our *own* free speech rights by voicing our objections to forms of expression that we don't like. Justice Louis Brandeis' advice that the remedy for messages we disagree with or dislike in art, entertainment or politics is "more speech, not enforced silence," is as true today as it was when given in 1927.

Further, we can exercise our prerogative as parents without resorting to censorship. Devices now exist that make it possible to block access to specific TV programs and internet sites. Periodicals that review books, recordings, and films can help parents determine what they feel is appropriate for their youngsters. Viewing decisions can, and should, be made at home, without government interference.

THE PRESS SHOULD BE RESTRICTED DURING THE WAR ON TERRORISM

Dennis Pluchinsky

Dennis Pluchinsky is a senior intelligence analyst specializing in terrorist threats with the Diplomatic Security Service in the U.S. Department of State. In the essay that follows, he expresses dismay at the lack of restraint shown by the news media, whom he accuses of exposing American vulnerabilities in national security during the war on terrorism. According to Pluchinsky, the publication of such information in the press can help terrorists learn how to be more effective. Therefore, he maintains, reporters should provide their findings about problems with national security privately to an appropriate government agency. Pluchinsky also recommends that the nation apply governmental restrictions on the freedom of the press similar to those implemented during World War II, arguing that such limitations on First Amendment rights are justified when the country is in crisis.

I accuse the media in the United States of treason. I have been analyzing terrorism for the U.S. government for 25 years. My specialty is "threat analysis." This is a rather difficult field that requires the imagination of Walt Disney, the patience of a kindergarten teacher, the mind-set of a chess player, the resolve of a Boston Red Sox fan, the mental acuity of a river boat gambler, and the forecasting ability of a successful stock market analyst.

Research Assistants for Terrorism

While the media have written extensively on alleged intelligence "failures" surrounding the events of Sept. 11 [2001], I want to address the media's common-sense "failures." As a terrorism analyst, I am both appalled and confused by many of the post-9/11 articles published at home and abroad, in newspapers, news magazines and academic journals, as well as on the Internet.

Many of these articles have clearly identified for terrorist groups the country's vulnerabilities—including our food supply, electrical grids, chemical plants, trucking industry, ports, borders, airports, special events and cruise ships. Some of these articles have been lengthy and have provided tactical details useful to terrorist groups. No terrorist group that I am aware of has the time and manpower to conduct this type of extensive research on a multitude of potential targets. Our news media, and certain think tankers and academicians, have done and continue to do the target vulnerability research for them.

Imagine that you are a supporter or sympathizer of a terrorist group and you have been tasked to identify and collect tactical information on potential U.S. targets. Consider some of the following headlines that have appeared since 9/11: "Private Plane Charters: One Way Around Air Security," "Suicidal Nuclear Threat Is Seen At Weapons Plants," "Priority Required for Protecting Utilities," "NRC Warns of Missing Radioactive Materials," "Freight Transport: Safe from Terror?" "Chemical Plants Are Feared As Targets," "America's Roads May Be Just As Vulnerable As Its Skies," "Study Assesses Risk of Attack on Chemical Plants," "Terror Risk Cited for Cargo Carried on Passenger Jets: 2 Reports List Security Gaps," and "Truck Terrorism Possible, U.S. Says: Investigation Finds Lack of Licensing Safeguards."

I do not understand the media's agenda here. This country is at war. Do you honestly believe that such stories and headlines, pointing out our vulnerabilities for Japanese and Nazi saboteurs and fifth columnists, would have been published during World War II? Terrorists gather targeting information from open sources and field surveillance. What other sources do they have? Do they have a multibillion-dollar intelligence community with thousands of employees? Do they have telecommunications satellites to intercept communications?

Terrorists Rely on Open Information

If there's one thing terrorists have been open about, it's their reliance on open information. In the mid-1980s there was a Belgian left-wing terrorist group called the Communist Combatant Cells, or CCC. At the time, it was carrying out a series of bombings against American targets in Belgium. The media there were speculating that the CCC had plants or spies inside various Belgian agencies to be able to carry out attacks so efficiently. "NATO Pipelines Sabotaged: Military Secrets in the Hands of the CCC?" read a headline in the Dec. 12, 1984, edition of the Belgian newspaper *Le Soir*. Finally, in a written communique disseminated in April 1985, the CCC explained how it acquired its targeting information. The communique stated: "Being methodical types and having considered the relative accessibility of the pipeline, we consulted the top-secret telephone book where, under 'Ministry of Defense,' every pumping station in the entire country is listed. We drew up our lists of all the towns these stations were located in, and decided to explore them during long walks in the countryside."

Terrorist groups continue to rely on open sources to come up with targeting ideas and tactical information. This is why the Internet has become so valuable to terrorist groups. Richard Clarke, head of the White House's Office of Cyberdefenses and probably the most knowledgeable high-level government official on terrorism, testified to Congress on Feb. 13 [2002], that, based on evidence found in the caves of Afghanistan, al Qaeda "was using the Internet to do at least reconnaissance of American utilities and American facilities." Furthermore, he noted, "if you put all the unclassified information together, sometimes it adds up to something that ought to be classified."

So why do the research for the terrorists? For example, "vulnerability" articles appearing in the media always contain interviews or comments from three or four experts or specialists. It could be the former head of the National Highway Traffic Safety Administration, an American Trucking Associations official, a union leader, technician or consultant. These experts will talk to reporters. None of them would ever talk to a terrorist. Therefore, if not for the media, terrorist groups would have no access to the insights and wisdom of these people. What also infuriates me is when the media publish follow-up reports noting that security measures or procedures around a specific target or system still have not been implemented. Not only do the media identify potential target vulnerabilities for the terrorists but they also provide our foes with progress reports!

In a war situation, it is not business as usual. Use some common sense. Certainly, if a reporter or academician believes that he or she has discovered a vulnerability or flaw in one of our sectors or systems, it is important to let others know. It seems reasonable to me that a process should be established where such articles are filtered through a government agency such as the proposed Department of Homeland Security. A skeptic would call this censorship; a patriot would call it cooperation. This type of cooperation existed during World War II and believe me, this current war is a "world war" also.

Pointing Out Mistakes to Terrorists

I also am concerned about the many articles detailing how the 9/11 terrorists were able to come and live in the United States. These articles have noted which mannerisms of the terrorists aroused the suspicion of their landlords, acquaintances, neighbors, flight instructors and others. Articles have pointed out what mistakes the terrorists made and how we failed to pick up on those mistakes. Al Qaeda terrorists now know to pay a speeding ticket promptly. They now know not to pay for things with large amounts of cash. They now know to buy some furniture for their apartments or rooms. They now know that they have to act friendly and not surly or antagonistic in their dealings with neighbors and other locals. They know now that they should have a phone installed in their apartments or rooms.

The U.S. media's autopsy of the movements and interactions of earlier terrorists may have helped the 9/11 hijackers and others seeking to come to the United States to do us harm. In a March 23 [2002], article entitled "The Jackals of Islam" that was published on an Islamic Web site, Abu-Ubayd al-Qurashi, believed to be a close aide to Osama bin Laden, commenting on the 9/11 operatives, stated that "the suicide hijackers studied the lives of Palestinian Yehiya Ayash [a Hamas bomb maker who was himself assassinated] and Ramzi Yousef [operational planner of the 1993 World Trade Center bombing] and the security mistakes that led to their downfall while they were preparing for the September 11 operation." How did al Qaeda know about the security mistakes that led to the death of Ayash and the capture of Yousef? The media, at home and abroad.

Courtrooms can also give terrorists windows into our thinking and methods. In the 1980s when German terrorists from the leftist Red Army Faction (RAF) were tried in Germany, the prosecution had to detail all of the evidence, including how they linked the terrorists to specific attacks. Forensic experts from the German BKA (comparable to the FBI) described in the open courtroom how they extracted fingerprints from items left at the attack sites. At the time, there were RAF sympathizers and supporters in the courtroom who took notes. It did not take long for the RAF terrorists still at large to change their methods—wearing gloves and spraying their hands with latex so that they would not leave any fingerprints.

The U.S. media are providing a similar service for al Qaeda. I am sure that al Qaeda will fix its mistakes and mannerisms before its next attack in the United States. I say the following with a heavy heart, but if there were an "Osama bin Laden" award given out by al Qaeda, I believe that it would be awarded to the U.S. news media for their investigative reporting. This type of reporting—carrying specifics about U.S. vulnerabilities—must be stopped or censored.

Proposals for Improvement

I propose that the Department of Homeland Security establish a program where academicians, reporters, think tankers or any citizen could contact the department and inform them of security vulnerabilities. If the department determined that these vulnerabilities indeed existed, then it could award "Homeland Security Protective Security" certificates to individuals or "Homeland Security Gold Stars" to newspaper or Internet sites that put the country first during a time of war. If displayed on its banner, this star might increase circulation.

During World War II, there was a security slogan that went: "Loose lips sink ships." Maybe the current security slogan should be: "Prolific pens propagate terrorist plots." The president and Congress should pass laws temporarily restricting the media from publishing any security information that can be used by our enemies. This was necessary during World War II, and it is necessary now. These restrictions were backed by the American public during World War II, and I believe the public would support them now.

As for "treason," well, maybe that accusation against the media is not justified. Webster's dictionary defines treason as violation of allegiance toward one's country and lists one of its characteristics as "consciously and purposely acting to aid its enemies." I know the media have not consciously and purposely aided al Qaeda. Therefore, *J'accuse* the media of lacking common sense. As a concerned terrorism analyst, I say the following to the media: You are making the jobs of terrorism analysts, intelligence officers and law enforcement officials very difficult. Help us, don't hinder us from defeating our enemies.

A FREE PRESS IS ESSENTIAL IN THE ERA OF TERRORISM

Paul McMasters

In the following article, Paul McMasters challenges the contention that in the fight against terrorism, freedom of the press is dangerous to national security. On the contrary, he insists, a free press increases the safety of American citizens by providing them with essential information about national vulnerabilities and the solutions proposed by leaders. Journalists help to pressure those charged with national security to be more accountable to the public, McMasters argues, and government censorship of the press would only serve to weaken this important function. McMasters is a longtime veteran of journalism and one of the nation's leading experts on freedom of the press. He is the First Amendment ombudsman for the Freedom Forum, a nonpartisan foundation dedicated to protecting free speech.

As usual, the nation's capital is leaking like a sieve. And administration officials are scrambling to track down and shut up government employees providing sensitive information to the enemy—that is to say, the press.

Defense Secretary Donald Rumsfeld has ordered an investigation into "criminal" leaks of information to newspapers about U.S. plans for a possible war against Iraq. The FBI has interrogated 39 members of Congress and their staffs, trying to find the source of a leak to the press about messages intercepted by the National Security Agency.

Blaming the Press

While the immediate targets are the leakers within government, it is the press that many government officials regard as the real problem. A defense official was quoted recently as saying: "We've got to do whatever it takes—if it takes sending SWAT teams into journalists' homes—to stop these leaks."

That, perhaps, was hyperbole in an unguarded moment. Not so an article by a federal intelligence analyst in [the June 16, 2002] issue of *The Washington Post*. "I accuse the media in the United States of treason." Dennis Pluchinsky wrote as the first sentence in the article.

This State Department official, criticizing news media coverage of possible targets of terrorists, went on to call for laws and policies restricting coverage of the war on terrorism.

"If there were an 'Osama bin Laden' award given out by al Qaeda," Pluchinsky wrote. "I believe that it would be awarded to the U.S. news media for their investigative reporting. This type of reporting—carrying specifics about U.S. vulnerabilities—must be stopped or censored."

Mr. Pluchinsky was voicing his own opinion, but it cannot be dismissed as isolated. In fact, there are many—inside and outside government—who regard the robust exercise of First Amendment rights by either the press or the people as a dangerous problem in the fight against terrorism.

Citing those concerns. Mr. Pluchinsky proposed that journalists filter any reporting on possible security problems through a government agency. And he called for the passage of laws "temporarily restricting the media from publishing any security information that can be used by our enemies."

Such proposals would make prior restraint the norm, self-censorship the ideal and democratic discourse an exercise in futility. They invoke two dangerous assumptions: 1) that the more accommodating the press, the more accountable the government, and 2) that the less Americans know, the safer they are.

Restrictions Since the September 11 Attacks

Further, they ignore a disturbing array of restrictions on the flow of information rushed into effect in the aftermath of [the terrorist attacks of] Sept. 11 [2001]. White House spokesman Ari Fleischer and National Security Adviser Condoleezza Rice called up television and newspaper executives to warn them about their coverage of Osama bin Laden. The State Department tried to suppress a Voice of America interview with the head of the Taliban. The Defense Department placed unprecedented restrictions on journalists attempting to cover the war in Afghanistan. The Justice Department closed immigration hearings and refused to release the names of detainees. Federal agencies removed information from their Web sites.

There were more direct restrictions on the press. In the ban on air traffic after Sept. 11, news media aircraft were kept grounded long after other private aircraft returned to the air. Photography was banned at the World Trade Center site. The Pentagon pre-empted news media use of satellite photos of the South Asia region. In addition, strict restrictions were placed on the ability of the press to cover the military operations in Afghanistan. At home, numerous restrictions on access to government information were put in place.

Even a national crisis is not sufficient justification for government officials to move so aggressively to constrict the flow of so much information to its citizens. Americans should keep in mind the news void concerning airport security flaws and the massive information-sharing failures—in federal agencies, congressional committees and the press—that left us lethally exposed to the horrors of 9-11.

Charging the press with irresponsibility or worse in reporting on our current vulnerabilities gives too much credence to the notion that terrorists would know nothing if it weren't for the news media. It breezes past the fact that much of the reporting on the war on terrorism relies heavily on leaks from federal agencies and Congress, as well as information provided by whistleblowers. And it fails to acknowledge that the press frequently has held or changed stories to prevent harm to national security or that it has engaged in a months-long dialogue with the intelligence community to address the problems that can arise from unauthorized leaks.

The Dangers of Censoring the Press

There is no question that the news media should exercise care. But Americans must recognize that being unaware of danger is not the same as being safe from danger. A critical component of our national security is knowing about our vulnerabilities and what our leaders are doing about them. Without the public pressure that unflinching journalism creates, vulnerabilities will remain for terrorists to exploit.

Then there is the problem of collateral damage to the First Amendment rights of others in proposing to restrict the press. Mr. Pluchinsky concedes as much by suggesting that there are other open sources that must be regarded as threats, such as courtroom proceedings, the academic community, think tanks, the Internet, even the telephone book.

We've been led down this road of the blind trust before. In other times of national crisis, we have surrendered rights and tolerated secrecy and censorship. We have punished political leaders, scholars, journalists and ordinary citizens for what they said and rounded up and interned thousands for who they were.

When we look back at those betrayals of our fundamental principles, we are embarrassed and not just a little unnerved. Even so, there are many among us—including some government officials—who still believe that we have no choice but to repeat those mistakes.

ORGANIZATIONS TO CONTACT

The editors have compiled the following list of organizations concerned with the issues presented in this book. The descriptions are derived from materials provided by the organizations. All have publications or information available for interested readers. The list was compiled on the date of publication of the present volume; the information provided here may change. Be aware that many organizations take several weeks or longer to respond to inquiries, so allow as much time as possible.

American Civil Liberties Union (ACLU)
125 Broad St., 18th Fl., New York, NY 10004
(212) 549-2500 • fax: (212) 549-2646
e-mail: aclu@aclu.org • website: www.aclu.org

The ACLU is a national organization that defends Americans' civil rights guaranteed in the U.S. Constitution. It adamantly opposes regulation of all forms of speech, including pornography and hate speech. The ACLU offers numerous reports, fact sheets, and policy statements on a wide variety of issues. Publications include the briefing papers "Freedom of Expression" and "Hate Speech on Campus" and the report "Freedom Under Fire: Dissent in Post–9/11 America."

American Library Association (ALA)
50 E. Huron St., Chicago, IL 60611
(800) 545-2433 • fax: (312) 440-9374
e-mail: ala@ala.org • website: www.ala.org

The ALA is the nation's primary professional organization for librarians. Through its Office for Intellectual Freedom (OIF), the ALA supports free access to libraries and library materials. The OIF also monitors and opposes efforts to ban books. The ALA's sister organization, the Freedom to Read Foundation, provides legal defense for libraries. Publications include the bimonthly *Newsletter on Intellectual Freedom*, articles, fact sheets, and policy statements, including "Freedom to Read Statement," and "Resolution Reaffirming the Principles of Intellectual Freedom in the Aftermath of Terrorist Attacks."

Canadian Association for Free Expression (CAFE)
PO Box 332, Station B, Etobicoke, ON M9W 5L3 Canada
(905) 897-7221 • fax: (905) 277-3914
e-mail: cafe@canadafirst.net • website: www.canadianfreespeech.com

CAFE, one of Canada's leading civil liberties groups, works to strengthen the freedom of speech and freedom of expression provisions in the Canadian Charter of Rights and Freedoms. It lobbies politicians and researches threats to freedom of speech. Publications include specialized reports, leaflets, and the *Free Speech Monitor*, which is published ten times per year.

Cato Institute
1000 Massachusetts Ave. NW, Washington, DC 20001-5403
(202) 842-0200 • fax: (202) 842-3490
e-mail: cato@cato.org • website: www.cato.org

The Cato Institute is a libertarian public policy research foundation. It advocates limited government and strongly opposes regulations on speech. The institute distributes books, policy papers, reports, and the triannual *Cato Journal*.

Concerned Women for America (CWA)

1015 Fifteenth St. NW, Suite 1100, Washington, DC 20005
(202) 488-7000 • fax: (202) 448-0806
e-mail: mail@cwfa.org • website: www.cwfa.org

CWA promotes conservative values and is concerned with creating an environment that is conducive to building strong families and raising healthy children. The organization advocates the use of Internet filters in schools and libraries and supports the passage of the Children's Internet Protection Act to block material that may be harmful to minors. CWA publishes the bimonthly *Family Voice* and numerous press releases and reports, including "Hard-Core Harm: Why You Can't Be Soft on Porn."

Electronic Frontier Foundation (EFF)

454 Shotwell St., San Francisco, CA 94110
(415) 436-9333 • fax: (415) 436-9993
e-mail: ask@eff.org • website: www.eff.org

EFF works to protect privacy and freedom of expression in the arena of computers and the Internet. Its missions include supporting litigation that protects First Amendment rights. EFF's website publishes an electronic bulletin, *Effector*, and the guidebook *Protecting Yourself Online: The Definitive Resource on Safety, Freedom, and Privacy in Cyberspace.*

Family Research Council (FRC)

801 G St. NW, Washington, DC 20001
(202) 393-2100 • fax: (202) 393-2134
e-mail: corrdept@frc.org • website: www.frc.org

The Family Research Council is an organization that believes pornography degrades women and children and seeks to strengthen current obscenity laws. It publishes the monthly newsletter *Washington Watch* and the bimonthly journal *Family Policy*, which features a full-length essay in each issue, such as "Keeping Libraries User and Family Friendly: The Challenge of Internet Pornography." The FRC also publishes policy papers, including "Indecent Proposal: The NEA Since the Supreme Court Decency Decision" and "Internet Filtering and Blocking Technology."

Freedom Forum

1101 Wilson Blvd., Arlington, VA 22209
(703) 528-0800 • fax: (703) 284-3770
e-mail: news@freedomforum.org • website: www.freedomforum.org

The Freedom Forum is a national organization that works to protect free speech and freedom of the press. It monitors developments in media and First Amendment issues on its website. The forum's First Amendment Center focuses on the study and exploration of free-expression issues. It publishes the annual report "State of the First Amendment," the teacher's guide *Free Speech and Music*, the report "Violence and the Media: An Exploration of Cause, Effect, and the First Amendment," and other studies and briefing papers.

Free Speech Coalition

PO Box 10480, Canoga Park, CA 91309
(800) 845-8503 • (818) 348-9373 • fax: (818) 886-5914
e-mail: freespeech@freespeechcoalition.com
website: www.freespeechcoalition.com

The Free Speech Coalition is a trade association that represents members of the adult entertainment industry. It seeks to protect the industry from attempts to censor pornography. Publications include fact sheets, *Free Speech X-Press*, and the report "The Truth About the Adult Entertainment Industry."

The Heritage Foundation
214 Massachusetts Ave. NE, Washington, DC 20002-4999
(800) 544-4843 • (202) 546-4400 • fax: (202) 546-8328
e-mail: info@heritage.org • website: www.heritage.org

The foundation is a conservative public policy organization dedicated to individual liberty, free-market principles, and limited government. It favors limiting freedom of the press when that freedom threatens national security. Its resident scholars publish position papers on a wide range of issues through publications such as the weekly *Backgrounder* and the bimonthly *Policy Review*.

Morality in Media (MIM)
475 Riverside Dr., Suite 239, New York, NY 10115
(212) 870-3222 • fax: (212) 870-2765
e-mail: mim@moralityinmedia.org • website: www.moralityinmedia.org

Morality in Media is an interfaith organization that fights pornography and opposes indecency in the mainstream media. It maintains the National Obscenity Law Center, a clearinghouse of legal materials on obscenity law. MIM publishes the bimonthlies *Morality in Media* and *Obscenity Law Bulletin* and several reports, including "Minors' Access to Pornography on the Internet Through Library and School Computers."

National Coalition Against Censorship (NCAC)
275 Seventh Ave., New York, NY 10001
(212) 807-6222 • fax: (212) 807-6245
e-mail: ncac@ncac.org • website: www.ncac.org

The coalition represents more than forty national organizations that work to prevent suppression of free speech and the press. NCAC educates the public about the dangers of censorship and how to oppose it. The coalition publishes the quarterly *Censorship News*, articles, various reports, and background papers. Papers include "Censorship's Tools Du Jour: V-Chips, TV Ratings, PICS, and Internet Filters" and "Free Speech in Wartime."

National Congress of Black Women (NCBW)
8484 Georgia Ave., Suite 420, Silver Spring, MD 20910
(877) 274-1198 • (301) 562-8000 • fax: (301) 562-8303
e-mail: info@npcbw.org • website: www.npcbw.org

The NCBW supports the advancement of African American women in politics and government. The congress also engages in research on critical issues that affect the quality of life of African American women and youth. Through its Commission on Entertainment, the NCBW campaigns against the glorification of violence, misogyny, pornography, and drugs in popular entertainment. It publishes project reports on its website, including "Crusading Against Gangsta/ Porno Rap."

People for the American Way (PFAW)
2000 M St. NW, Suite 400, Washington, DC 20036
(800) 326-7329 • (202) 467-4999 • fax: (202) 293-2672
e-mail: pfaw@pfaw.org • website: www.pfaw.org

PFAW works to promote citizen participation in democracy and safeguard the principles of the U.S. Constitution, including the right to free speech. It publishes a variety of fact sheets, articles, and position statements on its website and distributes the e-mail newsletter *Freedom to Learn Online*.

BIBLIOGRAPHY

Books

Randall P. Bezanson — *Speech Stories: How Free Can Speech Be?* New York: New York University Press, 1998.

Robert H. Bork — *Slouching Towards Gomorrah: Modern Liberalism and American Decline.* New York: Regan Books, 1996.

Ellen Henson Brinkley — *Caught Off Guard: Teachers Rethinking Censorship and Controversy.* Boston: Allyn and Bacon, 1999.

Tammy Bruce — *The New Thought Police: Inside the Left's Assault on Free Speech and Free Minds.* Roseville, CA: Forum, 2001.

Francis G. Couvares, ed. — *Movie Censorship and American Culture.* Washington, DC: Smithsonian Institution Press, 1996.

Richard Delgado and Jean Stefancic — *Must We Defend Nazis? Hate Speech, Pornography, and the New First Amendment.* New York: New York University Press, 1997.

June Edwards — *Opposing Censorship in the Public Schools: Religion, Morality, and Literature.* Mahwah, NJ: Lawrence Erlbaum Associates, 1998.

Marjorie Heins — *Not in Front of the Children: "Indecency," Censorship, and the Innocence of Youth.* New York: Hill and Wang, 2001.

Nat Hentoff — *Free Speech for Me—But Not for Thee: How the American Left and Right Relentlessly Censor Each Other.* New York: HarperCollins, 1992.

Nicholas J. Karolides, ed. — *Censored Books II: Critical Viewpoints, 1985–2000.* Lanham, MD: Scarecrow Press, 2002.

Sheila Suess Kennedy, ed. — *Free Expression in America: A Documentary History.* Westport, CT: Greenwood Press, 1999.

Kathryn Kolbert and Zak Mettger — *Censoring the Web.* New York: The New Press, 2001.

David Lowenthal — *No Liberty for License: The Forgotten Logic of the First Amendment.* Dallas: Spence, 1997.

Charles Lyons — *The New Censors: Movies and the Culture Wars.* Philadelphia: Temple University Press, 1997.

Eric Nuzum — *Parental Advisory: Music Censorship in America.* New York: Perennial, 2001.

Robert S. Peck — *Libraries, the First Amendment, and Cyberspace: What You Need to Know.* Chicago: American Library Association, 2000.

Louise S. Robbins — *Censorship and the American Library: The American Library Association's Response to Threats to Intellectual Freedom, 1939–1969.* Westport, CT: Greenwood Press, 1996.

Timothy C. Shiell   *Campus Hate Speech on Trial.* Lawrence: University
                             Press of Kansas, 1998.

John S. Simmons   *School Censorship in the 21st Century: A Guide for
and Eliza T. Dresang   Teachers and School Library Media Specialists.* Newark,
                             DE: International Reading Association, 2001.

Ann K. Symons and   *Speaking Out! Voices in Celebration of Intellectual
Sally Gardner Reed,   Freedom.* Chicago: American Library Association,
eds.   1999.

Jonathan Wallace and   *Sex, Laws, and Cyberspace: Freedom and Censorship on
Mark Mangan   the Frontiers of the Online Revolution.* New York: Henry
                             Holt, 1997.

Periodicals

Andrew Brown   "The Limits of Freedom," *New Statesman*, February 12,
                             1999.

Conscience   "Index: A Selective Timeline of Censorship,
                             1235–2003," Spring 2003. Available from 1436 U St.
                             NW, Suite 301, Washington, DC 20009-3997.

Michael Cromartie   "Give Me Liberty, but Don't Give Me Filth,"
                             Christianity Today, May 19, 1997.

Emily Eakin   "The Censor and the Artists: A Murky Border," *New
                             York Times*, November 26, 2002.

Economist   "Banned Music," November 28, 1998.

Stephen Goode   "Censorship on College Campuses," *Insight on the
                             News*, June 3, 2002. Available from 3600 New York
                             Ave. NE, Washington, DC 20002.

Linda Greenhouse   "Sides Debate Web Access in Libraries," *New York
                             Times*, March 6, 2003.

Irving Kristol   "Liberal Censorship and the Common Culture,"
                             Society, September/October 1999.

David Lowenthal   "The Case for Censorship," *Weekly Standard*, August
                             23, 1999. Available from 1150 17th St. NW, Suite 505,
                             Washington, DC 20036-4617.

Jay Nordlinger   "Getting Aroused: What It Takes to Combat Porn,"
                             National Review, November 19, 2001.

Sara Paretsky   "The New Censorship," *New Statesman*, June 2, 2003.

Anna Quindlen   "With a No. 2 Pencil, Delete: The Destruction of
                             Literature in the Name of Children," *Newsweek*, June
                             17, 2002.

Roxana Robinson   "Censorship or Common Sense?" *New York Times*,
                             October 19, 1998.

Brian Siano   "Tales from the Crypt," *Humanist*, March/April 1994.

Max J. Skidmore   "Censorship: Who Needs It? How the Conventional
                             Wisdom Restricts Information's Free Flow," *Journal of
                             Popular Culture*, Winter 2001.

Patrick J. Sloyan   "This Is War: Hiding Bodies: How the White House
                           Makes Sure That Members of the Press Don't End Up
                           Showing You Anything Too Upsetting," *Rolling Stone*,
                           March 20, 2003.

Stuart Taylor Jr.   "How Campus Censors Squelch Freedom of Speech,"
                           National Journal, July 12, 2003. Available from 1501 M
                           St. NW, #300, Washington, DC 20005.

Bernard A. Weisberger   "Chasing Smut in Every Medium," *American Heritage*,
                           December 1997.

Jonathan Yardley   "Read No Evil: A Textbook Case of Censorship,"
                           Washington Post, June 12, 2003.

Charles M. Young   "Censure and Censorship," *Billboard*, November 1,
                           1994. Available from 770 Broadway, New York, NY
                           10003.

INDEX